From Green to ESG:

How Data-Driven Transparency Changed Real Estate for Good

By Matt Ellis

To my family, friends, mentors, investors, and customers who believe in measuring what matters.

Table of Contents

Foreword by David L. Pogue

Former Global Director of Corporate Responsibility at CBRE

Much like my friend and former colleague, Matt Ellis, I became involved in sustainability by chance and circumstance. In the spring of 2006, I was overseeing property management for the western region of CBRE, the largest commercial real estate services company in the world. Energy costs were rising, and I led a small group of colleagues seeking ways to assist our clients in reducing their use. This would save money, which was always in our client's interest, and coincidentally also create an environmental win. This was becoming more important as the conversation about climate change and carbon was heating up.

We introduced the requirement for all large office buildings to participate in the EPA ENERGY STAR program and introduced a broader program aimed at improving the sustainability performance of those buildings, including among other things recycling, training, tenant engagement, and client communication that we called the Standards of Sustainability. Taken together, we called the program *Sensible Sustainability*. Within a few weeks we had more than 125 people throughout the company helping with our efforts, encouraging their colleagues, and suggesting new ideas for us to adopt and promote. We were now fully launched, and our managers and engineers were engaged.

Our work coincided with events occurring at the company level. By 2007, Corporate Responsibility was taking form and CBRE created a committee of internal and external leaders to study the issue and make recommendations for action. I was included in that original group because of the sustainability work we were doing in property management. The outcome of the committee's work was a commitment to review and publish our current status on a range of environmental, employee, and community issues in an annual

Corporate Social Responsibility Report and to seek continually better results in key metrics. We also made a commitment to be carbon neutral by 2010, the first such commitment by a real estate services company. To cap it off, I was named the company's first Global Director of Sustainability.

It was around this time that I met an ambitious and passionate young industrial broker from San Diego, Matt Ellis. Our meeting was also by chance and circumstance. Matt already had expressed interest in sustainability. He also had a wild and impractical idea involving carbon capture in a tract of South American rainforest. I had an interest in carbon offsets as we already knew the only way we were going to achieve carbon neutrality was through the purchase of offsets. The rainforest carbon capture idea proved unproductive—but the meeting with Matt was.

In time Matt would join my team as a sustainability consultant, soon to advance to Global Director of Sustainability Solutions. Perhaps not surprisingly, one of his first assignments was acquiring the offsets needed to meet our original commitment. Another of his initial assignments was overseeing the data collection and submission for a client's first GRESB report. During that tedious process, he saw not only his own future but that of our industry.

I, like most others in the field, was an old school manager, relying on consultive solutions and narratives. Matt immediately recognized something that eluded me and many of my peers: the scope and complexity of the issue was too vast for old approaches. Digitization, timely dashboards, and objective metrics were needed. The data would become the narrative. What you measure, you can manage. The core concept behind Measurabl was born.

The industry has come a long way from those early days when an ENERGY STAR, LEED or BREEAM label alone conferred status. There have been numerous "gold standard" designations and certifications that each in time has been surpassed by the next, each claiming to be more transparent, timely, and objective. But the demands for more action, better outcomes, and more data continue to grow.

As "Green" became "ESG", the issues have become more complex, the expectations larger and more specific, and the cost of failure higher. The story told in the following pages illustrates this. But most importantly, it also shows that the story of ESG is not fully written. Every day, new topics like decarbonization, climate resilience, health and wellness, and DEI take on greater importance and require new data sets, tools, and approaches.

I am confident the new generation of sustainability leaders, among whom Matt sits prominently, will be driven by pursuit of environmental and social good and guided by data. In doing so, they will continue the industry progress in which I was fortunate to have played a part.

Introduction

My commercial real estate career began in January 2008. It's a time best known as the start of the Great Financial Crisis—a crisis originating in the real estate sector. It's also the date I started my job as a broker at CBRE, the world's largest commercial real estate services company. Obviously, my timing was not ideal. But I was young and unaware of the magnitude of the financial collapse, so I showed up for my first day on the job as bright eyed as any fresh recruit.

My positive attitude was tested in the first few minutes.

When I reached the lobby entrance, I paused to hold the door for a person carrying a fully loaded cardboard box. But it was the look on her face that left no doubt: my first day on the job was this person's last. The real estate market was in meltdown.

By the time I reached the elevator I knew that if I wanted to survive— let alone succeed—it wouldn't be with the traditional real estate skillset. I needed to differentiate myself and create new value in a market this challenging. Otherwise, I'd be carrying my own cardboard box sooner rather than later.

Those early days were extremely difficult. Vacancy rates were skyrocketing. Bankrupt tenants were breaking leases. Property values were plummeting as defaults and foreclosures rose. Layoffs were brisk.

By June, I had taken to a regular schedule of looking for clients by knocking on doors in the Poway Industrial Park, a bland grid of multi-tenant buildings 22 miles northeast of downtown San Diego. I was pounding the pavement on one mercilessly hot day when I noticed a decal on the door of one nondescript building. It read "ENERGY STAR Certified."

No doubt I had seen a decal like this before but, on that hot day, I lingered in the shade of the building's awning and for the first time wondered what the insignia actually meant. Why had the landlord put it there? What did it signal to prospective tenants? Who issued the certification?

Back in the office that afternoon—no deals in hand and trying to look busy for my managers—I googled "ENERGY STAR building." It led me down the rabbit hole that has since consumed my professional life.

That search was the first time I heard of "Green buildings." That there were "brown" buildings, and by contrast, "Green" ones were supposed to be more profitable for investors, healthier for tenants, and better for our shared environment. It resonated with me. My environmental awareness was instilled by my mom at an early age, but it had never occurred to me that passion could have a place in my professional life. Maybe "Green" buildings were the differentiating angle I'd been looking for?

Commercial real estate is considered a hard-nosed profession. In fact, after closing a particularly large industrial deal despite the recession, my mentor, Tom Martinez, looked at me and said, "this business is legalized gambling." We had been dealt a good hand that month, he explained, but the months to come could be just as bleak as the several before.

But real estate is ultimately also an incredibly pragmatic business. The goals are clear: maximize tenancy and rental rates, control operating expenses, create stable yield with operational *nous* and embrace the fact that a degree of luck aka "the market" will (hopefully) do the rest. After six months of this equation being pounded into my head it finally struck me as missing a variable: sustainability.

After all, tenancy could be improved by offering healthy environments for workers. Operating expenses could be reduced through energy efficiency measures, with carbon reduction a charismatic byproduct. Preserving the value of physical assets could be accomplished in part by increasing their resilience to climate shocks like floods or wildfire. In other words, all the same variables in the equation remained but each could be multiplied by a "sustainability coefficient."

That night I wrote a memo about how CBRE could radically extend its market leadership by offering a comprehensive set of sustainability solutions. I sent it to my boss, Mark Read, and up the chain it went. I look back now and am still a bit embarrassed by my presumption that anyone would care about the "sustainability coefficient." But it resonated.

The next few months went by in a flash. I was encouraged to build the proposition by senior leaders at CBRE. A new Sustainability Practice Group was created, and I became its co-chair, along with a few wonderful colleagues who shared my vision that sustainability could positively transform the way the real estate business worked. The practice group evangelized the merits of sustainability and educated brokers on its practical implications in their leasing business. Two years later I was elevated to Director of Sustainability Solutions, the company's first. My personal and professional interests combined and my aspiration to differentiate myself professionally had come true.

In the decade since, my conviction in sustainability's importance to real estate has only increased. In those early years, the tools for defining a building's sustainability performance were limited to whether or not it was certified by one of many Green building standards. The U.S. EPA's ENERGY STAR program for buildings was stood up in 1992. LEED certification was created a year later. In the decades since, these and many other certifications became the best proxy real estate professionals and their customers had for how Green or not a building was. They played an important, if ultimately limited role in the evolution from Green to ESG by raising awareness of the need for, and definition of, sustainability in real estate.

In the last few years, we've seen another, more seismic, advancement. The importance of sustainability and ESG (environmental, social, and governance) metrics for real estate investing has taken center stage. This is a radical departure from simply certifying a building as "Green" or "not Green" and calling it a day. Instead, the industry began to recognize there was no such thing as a "Green" or "brown" building. Every building on Earth exists on a spectrum. ESG, and the metrics behind it, help real estate owners measure the location of an asset or portfolio on that spectrum and act accordingly.

Once thought of as fluffy, nice-to-have ideals, ESG and sustainability have been endorsed as *the right way* to evaluate business—especially in real estate. They proved to be effective leading indicators of an asset and portfolio's financial prospects. Simply put: the more sustainable an investment, the better it would likely perform.

Institutional investors have taken note. Last year Larry Fink, CEO of BlackRock—the world's largest asset manager—told shareholders that sustainability had become the firm's new standard for selecting investments. To Fink, it's simple: "A company's prospects for growth are inextricable from its ability to operate sustainably... Actions that damage society will catch up with a company and destroy shareholder value."

Fink and business leaders like him have come to a consensus that the business was missing something in the way that it measured performance. The Miltonian doctrine that corporations exist to maximize shareholder value alone (distilled to share price) was deemed to be financially myopic.

There's no debate that real estate is a capital-intensive business with profit as its main motive. That will not change. The industry takes in dollars to produce brick and mortar boxes in which residents live (multifamily), workers labor (offices), and services, like cloud computing, are rendered (data centers). The costs to building and operating those boxes is more than the upfront cash, or ongoing maintenance that accrue over decades, or even centuries a building exists. There are environmental and social costs as well. Historically, those were not factored into the real estate equation.

Since the energy crisis of the 1970s, real estate companies have been looking for alternatives to increasingly expensive fossil fuels. As climate change has increased the risk of floods, fires, and violent storms, developers have sought ways to mitigate these risks. Now, as economies struggle to recover from the COVID-19 pandemic, building owners are searching for ways to make homes and workplaces healthier. There is nothing new in the desire to lower costs, mitigate risk, operate a business in perpetuity, and attract investors.

But for markets to work perfectly, they require perfect information. And the real estate industry is no different.

We've come a long way from those early notions of Green real estate. For decades, what it meant to be "Green" was nebulous and the data to back it up was opaque. ESG today is an altogether different proposition. Spurred on by new technologies that make it possible to acquire, interpret, and apply ESG data, and propelled by the demands of sophisticated investors who demand insight into the true risks of real estate investing, ESG represents an evolution in the business and an imperative.

I see a lot of real estate owners coming to ESG because they're worried capital providers may penalize them. But it's more existential than that. If you're unable to measure, manage, report and act on ESG, you will be out of business in ten years time. What was once subjective, warm and fuzzy, nice-to-have—that is all now objective and essential. Real estate owners need to change their game and embrace the ESG Era. Their survival is on the line.

Chapter 1:

The Transformation to Sustainable Real Estate

Let's start at the very beginning. Real estate is a market of information. The more information you have, the more likely you are to succeed in that market. To that end, **Environmental, Social, and Governance** (ESG) information is crucial for identifying the overall value and potential of a real estate asset and the portfolios they comprise.

To understand the importance of ESG to the real estate sector requires first establishing the link between the goals of real estate investors and the information their surrogates, like brokers, use in their decision-making process. Here's why...

Whether it's commercial or residential real estate, the difference between a good or a bad investment really comes down to just three things—and no, those three things aren't "location, location, location."

Location is, of course, the first factor people consider: Is it in the right town, suburb, or street? If the investor is looking for a residential property: What are the schools like nearby? How convenient is public transportation? Will sunlight shine into the bedrooms in the early morning? What's the view like? If they're shopping for a commercial opportunity, buyers will want to know the economics of the community, information about other commercial buildings in the vicinity, tenancy rates in the local area, and so on.

But location isn't as simple as that. As climate changes over time, the location question requires an understanding of the rising risks of natural disasters like flooding, wildfires, droughts, and extreme storms. Buyers want to know if they're buying into a flood zone or into the path of the next big hurricane. Beyond regional geographic trends, location can make a difference even at the local level. Just a small rise in elevation can protect a property against flash floods, and the position of a building can make it more resistant to strong winds.

The second consideration is the **value** of the property. How much is the house, apartment building, retail space, or office tower worth? Beyond simply ensuring you don't pay too much for a poor-quality property, the accuracy of the valuation has a range of financial implications. It determines insurance costs and taxation. It will influence financing terms and the potential income you will be able to earn from the investment.

There are any number of valuation approaches—from considering the cost to rebuild from scratch, to comparing the property to other recent sales, from value per gross rent, to calculating the income an investor can derive from a given property. But any calculation is only as good as the numbers behind it—the data inputs for the valuation. Institutional investors consider a multitude of factors that aren't known to the market at large, or they make use of historical data in sophisticated proprietary ways designed to give the investor an edge over the competition. The sheer quantity of data available to real estate valuers has grown exponentially in the last decade, as public records are digitized, and third parties build up their own databases of historical prices and other elements.

Yet historical prices are still only half of the valuation story. Useful valuations also take into consideration other factors to determine likely future pricing. A big part of this calculation involves how climatic and environmental factors may impact future valuations. An easy example of this consideration in action is a house built near an eroding cliff. How quickly is the cliff eroding, and will its erosion eventually claim the property the investor intends to buy? There are many other salient examples, such as shifting wildfires and extreme weather patterns.

Valuations also fluctuate depending on a building's adherence to government regulations or uptake of government subsidies and tax breaks. If a building's boiler does not operate to emissions codes, the building is less valuable. If it has solar energy panels which feed back into the grid, it may be more valuable.

Beyond the initial valuation, real estate investors also need to take running costs into consideration when buying or leasing a property. For instance, localized rises in the average temperature impact ongoing energy and water costs. Depending on a particular asset's energy and water efficiency, it will be more or less valuable over the long term. The more measures that are put in place to reduce these costs, the more valuable the property is to prospective investors.

The third general component of a good real estate investment is **how close the investment's purpose matches** what the buyer wants to do with the property. To match goals with opportunities is yet another complex equation, and investors usually have multiple—often conflicting—objectives when they approach an opportunity. But to put it simply, if a buyer is looking for a family home on a farm, it probably won't fit their purpose to buy a retail storefront in the city.

In commercial real estate, there are six basic categories of investment purpose:

1. Buy to use yourself

2. Lease to use yourself

3. Buy to lease out

4. Lease to sublease

5. Buy with a view to selling short term

6. Buy and hold to sell down the line

An investor's goals drive their decision-making. Their goals will be a balance of short-term needs versus long-term objectives. Does the investor want to generate income, build equity, or use the building themselves? The investor must analyze the data available to judge the investment opportunity by its ability to meet their goals and objectives.

Location. Valuation. Fit for purpose.

In practice, real estate operates like any other market. The savvy seller will try to convince the buyer that the property fits their overall needs, while the astute buyer will try to counter these claims—either to assure themselves the investment fits their objectives, or to cross the property off their list of options. Rinse and repeat.

The experienced real estate professional might find the above description of their business overly simplistic. And it absolutely is. There are nuances to location, valuation, and purpose that I did not describe in detail, and there are myriad considerations I did not cover (leverage and cash flow, for starters). However, the description serves to underline an important point: Real estate is a market of *information.*

Those who have it, succeed. Those who don't, fail.

There are rules, of course, to how this information market is governed. Generally, sellers have a duty to disclose hazards and defects that they know to be present on the property. If a buyer asks a question, the seller cannot outright lie. Yet much risk exists in the gulf between what a seller discloses and what the buyer assumes. The "winner" of the deal is the person with the most accurate data.

This idea is not new. It is one that governs all forms of commerce. The more complex the market, the more information is required to make a decision. Information is the fuel that drives capital markets, and there are strict rules about the disclosure of financial information. Listed companies must publish their financials in a timely and public way. They must provide full, honest, and regular disclosures of their company's revenue, liabilities, assets, and operations. Why? So that investors and the market at large can make informed decisions that take into consideration the positive and the negative aspects of an investment opportunity—unfiltered by subjective opinion or spin.

Free and unfiltered access to information is a basic requirement of a healthy and efficient market. When there is a lack of information, the market breaks down and participants are unable to make informed decisions. Bernie Madoff—America's most infamous Ponzi scheme operator—was a master of concealment. He made his money by sleight of hand, enshrouding his operations in secrecy and making fraudulent claims to the market. It was not until sunlight was cast on his dishonesty that his crimes were discovered.[1]

Sunlight is the best disinfectant.

Information fuels the capital markets, but what an investor chooses to do with that information is up to them. They may choose to ignore it, acting on their instinct or a hunch. They may make the wrong play, but the reasons for their decisions should not be for lack of available information. They must have the ability to understand and dissect the information or they risk making bad calls. The masters of the capital markets—the big investment banks and hedge fund managers—are those who can react smarter and faster to the information available, or those who can unearth information that their competitors do not have. Better, *faster* use of information is their greatest advantage.

Late to the party but here at last

The real estate market is no different, but it has come late to information transparency. And it came kicking and screaming. It is worth remembering that the natural inclination of the seller or broker is to put themselves in the best position to make the deal that is best for them. I say this not as an uninformed cynic, but as a former broker with years of experience. The real estate business has always been built on opacity.

As a broker, it was only because I worked at a large firm that was engaged in thousands of transactions a year that I had market insight into demand and value of assets. Information was our edge. There is no stock exchange for real estate. Perfect markets require perfect information,[2] but in the real estate market, transparency does not happen by design. Brokers do not want buyers or sellers to have perfect information because their goal is to arbitrage their opponent's inability to fully understand the particulars of an investment opportunity relative to the market.

Market opacity forces sellers to hire a broker to help them obtain the best deal. On the buy-side, it is equally difficult to shop for real estate without an intermediary to help them navigate the market. To find out what properties are available requires a professional broker. Even with the advent of online markets, such Zillow and Redfin, it is often the case that the best residential properties still go unlisted or cannot be accessed without a broker. This is especially true with commercial opportunities, even after the launch of commercial listing services like Costar.

The digitization of listings was an important development in the transparency of the real estate market, providing investors with the ability to know what has been bought and sold, and for how much. Technology has brought greater transparency to price, and it is inching its way to other parts of the real estate industry as well.

Services such as Zillow and Redfin allow market participants to view the market as a whole and quickly obtain detailed information about particular opportunities. 3D imaging and floor plans allow buyers to walk through properties and obtain a feel for the space. Tables of historical prices help them track the value of a property at the click of a mouse. Here lies the actual reason the real estate industry resisted "going digital" for so long: because online marketplaces created transparency in areas where previously brokers were able to arbitrage ignorance.

But the long arc of market evolution is moving real estate further toward transparency. The Zillows of the world are only the beginning because sellers will always be looking for an edge, and buyers will search for a way to improve their understanding of investment opportunities. Transparency is an unstoppable force.

The information flood brought on by online real estate marketplaces has quickly been utilized to better titrate the flow of capital based on improved transparency of price and the elements that make up a valuation. But investors are learning that price is not the end of the story. To create an edge over the competition, smart participants want as much information as they can consume. ESG is increasingly being seen by real estate investors as an important part of this edge, taking their cues from other geographic markets and other industries.

Long before ESG indicators emerged as a method for evaluating real estate assets, these non-financial metrics had gained traction in the equity markets. First by institutional investors such as endowments and sovereign wealth funds, and then by ultra-wealthy, multigenerational families. These sophisticated investors concluded that ESG was material information that provided them with a way to better understand the risk and potential reward of an investment opportunity.[3] While some market participants may not agree with this principle (or they simply may not believe in ESG), the market has spoken. ESG is here to stay.

Building the complete picture

ESG indicators are just as important as financial data (such as annual statements) in assessing a company's health because they provide a more complete picture of a company's operations, risks, and potential over the long term.[4] Along with traditional financial data, ESG provides investors with even more information with which to make decisions. Accurate reading of this information creates an edge over the competition.

A poignant capital markets example of ESG indicators unearthing good equities and flagging risk is the fashion sector. The manufacture of clothing and textiles is a highly energy-consuming, materials-heavy, labor-intensive business. The constant pressure to reduce costs forces manufacturers to find ways to reduce energy consumption, switch to sustainable material supplies, and seek cheaper globalized labor. Fashion companies regularly overhaul their manufacturing processes to use less energy and less water so that they can improve overheads. They are constantly searching for alternatives to traditional materials, such as replacing increasingly expensive cowhide with innovations in plant-based leather and synthetic materials.

Clothing companies carefully monitor their international labor forces to ensure their operations do not fall foul of human trafficking prohibitions and health and safety protections. Fashion-conscious consumers reward brands that follow sustainability practices[5]—and in turn, the capital flows in their direction.[6]

Product demand in the fashion business is also entirely at the mercy of the tastes and preferences of the increasingly discerning consumer. The market will punish brands whose operations are contrary to commonly held values, such as bans on child labor and cruelty to animals.

Whether an investor agrees with the underlying principles of ESG—that protecting the environment and society is a business imperative—is essentially irrelevant to the pragmatic rationale for using ESG data. When a savvy investor chooses a clothing industry stock, they will take ESG data into consideration because it is a leading indicator of a fashion brand's ability to attract customers and sustain long-term success. Perhaps more importantly, ESG criteria can flag high risk fashion companies that do not comply with the market's standards—for instance, companies that are not ethically sourcing their materials and will therefore run afoul of industry regulations and their customers' values.[7]

Far more than quarterly financial filings, ESG indicators can help investors identify stocks that are adhering to practices which will ensure the ongoing long-term success of the investment.[8] ESG data is complementary to financial information when making an investment decision.

When combined, financials and ESG information provide a holistic view of an equity's performance and potential. Studies have shown that the majority of ESG funds outperform the wider market over a 10-year period.[9] As a result, institutional investors place a premium on stocks that can prove their ESG credentials.

It can be argued that when it comes to large physical assets such as real estate, this premise is even more sound, because environmental and social factors are particularly germane to the places in which we live and work. Real estate is a resource-hungry industry. It consumes a tremendous number of raw materials. Deloitte estimates that inclusive of construction and operation, the building sector alone contributes to 40 percent of global carbon emissions.[10] A building that implements an effective solar energy solution will, over time, reduce its reliance on expensive fossil fuels. The same is true for properties that utilize smart thermostats to regulate heating and cooling; their lower energy usage and carbon emissions can reduce tax exposure and overall costs. These are just two examples of how ESG indicators can help investors obtain a deeper view of an asset. However, these formulas only work if the investor has access to accurate data. The better we are at measuring ESG, the better the market can direct the flow of capital into sound investments.

But we haven't always been good at it. And sometimes we've been objectively bad.

From "Green" to ESG

The path between where we are—and where we are going—with ESG takes us from the embryonic aspirations of "Green" construction in the mid-1800s to the development of sustainability principles in the 1980s, on to the rise of Corporate Social Responsibility (CSR) as a management ethos, and then finally to the emergence of ESG as a framework of quantifying hitherto unquantifiable aspects of a real estate property. It is not a direct path. There are conceptual overlaps at every step. Seen through the lens of Green-with-a-capital-G's contribution to our understanding of an asset's health, it is a fascinating tale that helps us comprehend the insight that can be gleaned from the ESG data available today.

Modern concepts of Green building can be traced back to the mid-19th Century, when construction of London's Crystal Palace—a giant plate glass structure built to house the Great Exhibition of 1851—utilized underground air-cooling chambers and rooftop ventilators to regulate temperature. By the early 20th Century, buildings such as New York's Flatiron and Chicago's Carson Pirie Scott department store (now the Sullivan Center) featured deep-set windows to shade the sun and retractable awnings to regulate interior temperatures and reduce energy costs.[11]

The overriding goal of these early developments was to improve conditions within built environments and to lower the costs of property operation and maintenance. They were not necessarily intended to save the environment.

Britain's Building Research Establishment was founded in 1921 as a national laboratory to improve the quality of housing in the UK after the First World War. Its purview included researching how heating and insulation improved quality of life and energy costs for the average citizen. By 1949, it was investigating the impact of the British climate on construction materials. As well as improving habitability and reducing cost, BRE was also tasked with bettering the sustainability of Britain's construction resources from a purely economic standpoint, albeit with no consistent notion of environmental impact as we understand it today.[12]

Our contemporary notion of Green building has its roots in the environmental movement of the 1960s; however, it crystallized during the oil crisis of the 1970s. By 1973, an embargo of the United States, imposed by the Organization of the Petroleum Exporting Countries

(OPEC), led to supply shortages of gasoline and skyrocketing fossil fuel prices. Americans, sick of long lines to fill their gas tanks and steep hikes in energy bills, began to question the country's reliance on oil and began wondering about the alternatives.[13]

Around the same time, the American Institute of Architects was investigating how factors like reflective roofing materials, triple-glazed windows, and building positioning could achieve energy savings. Certain members of the AIA were experimenting with alternative building materials and designs to improve insulation and energy consumption. In 1973, the AIA formed an energy committee to lobby the U.S. government for building guidelines that incorporated environmental and energy considerations. Much of the federal and state regulatory frameworks for energy and environmental standards for buildings that date back to the 1970s are based on the AIA's early research.[14]

By the 1990s, the real estate industry was taking steps to institutionalize the concept of Green building and quantify what it meant to be Green. The tool of choice in these early years was assessing buildings against set criteria and subsequently certifying a property's "greenness."

By 1988 in the UK, the BRE had created the Building Research Establishment Environmental Assessment Method (BREEAM), launching it in January 1990 as a voluntary assessment and certification process, which went beyond environmental regulations of the time. BREEAM is now the world's longest established sustainability assessment methodology for the built environment.

A few years later, the U.S. Green Building Council (USGBC) partnered with the Natural Resources Defense Council (NRDC) to create a certification process for the American building industry, and by 1998 they had developed the LEED—Leadership in Energy and Environmental Design—program. LEED certification is based on a point system. Candidate buildings must prove certain prerequisites and minimum requirements to qualify for one of four levels of certification: Certified, Silver, Gold, and Platinum.

Even as concepts of Green building evolved through the 1970s and 1990s, real estate investors could not easily find actionable information that could help them make sound investment decisions. If an investor knew what type of electrical and climate control infrastructure a building had, they could roughly work out if the building's energy bills might be higher or lower than average. However, they would need to investigate this themselves, since there was no central repository for information. They would need to somehow ascertain the average bill of a comparable property if they had any hopes of benchmarking this data.

If an investor could deduce that an asset contravened environmental rules, they might be able to determine the potential risk of regulatory penalties, and the subsequent knock to its bottom line. However, short of conducting their own probe, such contravention would be difficult for an investor to establish until it was too late to incorporate into their decision-making.

The Green Era was laudable for its ambitious intentions and the creation of a new way of thinking about real estate. What the creation of this new Green qualifier truly encouraged was for market participants to do good and be transparent about the totality of their business. However, it provided no uniform way to measure or compare buildings against each other, save for the binary observation that either a building was Green or it was not Green. The information of the era did not provide actionable insight that investors could use to conduct due diligence on an investment opportunity.

Worse still, Green-with-a-capital-G took a detour that arguably set back our ability to measure greenness by a couple of decades.

Greenwashing: From 'nice-to-have' to cynical claim

The U.S. Environmental Protection Agency defines Green building as "the use of approaches that create buildings and development that are environmentally responsible and resource-efficient throughout a building's life cycle, from site selection to demolition or reuse."[15]

It certainly sounds like a good thing to do. But how do you measure it? If a property claims it is Green, how can you quantify those claims? And what do developers even mean by Green? This was the problem the real estate market found itself grappling with at the turn of the 21st Century.

The gap between perception and reality of Green in the real estate market was caused in part by a wider problem society was facing: Greenwashing.

In 1983, when environmentalist Jay Westerveld was traveling through the South Pacific, he found a small notice in the room of a beach resort in Fiji. The notice asked that for the sake of the environment and to conserve precious water, guests could reuse their towels instead of having them laundered every day. To Westerveld, who noticed the resort was embarking on an expensive expansion at the time, the plea struck him as self-serving and hypocritical. He felt the proprietors were more interested in saving money rather than the ecosystem.[16]

By coining the phrase greenwashing, Westerveld was putting a name to a practice that was at least as old as the environmental movement itself. As far back as the 1960s, corporations were making unfounded or overblown claims about their environmental practices in a bid to wash over their transgressions and ride the popularity of the Green movement.

One famous example was oil company Chevron's 1980s "People Do" ad campaign, which featured Chevron employees protecting butterflies, bears, and other charming animals—all while the company was openly violating the Clean Air and Clean Water Acts and polluting wildlife refuges.

Another was forestry company Weyerhaeuser, which ran a campaign promoting the importance of caring for fish while its operations were destabilizing salmon habitats.

This phenomenon of "eco-exaggeration" refers to corporate advertising or labels that use Green messages when their products have little or no positive environmental benefits, or their Green claims are so vague that it is difficult to determine their actual value. It is the act of misleading consumers about a company's environmental practices or the Green benefits of a product, service, or building.[17] It is through this lens of cynical advertising that the public viewed much of the early attempts that corporations made to improve the environmental impact of their activities. But greenwashing has been far more endemic and widespread.

The story of emissions trading, carbon markets, and carbon offsetting is a good case in point.

Emissions trading—or cap-and-trade, as it is commonly known—is an approach to controlling pollution based on market forces. Emissions markets are created so that the ability to pollute becomes a tradable commodity. The goal is to use market forces to make polluting expensive and therefore financially punish participants who pollute— and reward those who don't. In the U.S., the system became law in 1990 to curb power-plant pollutants which were throwing sulfur dioxide into the atmosphere, causing acid rain which damaged forests and lakes across North America.[18]

Emissions markets work by providing market participants with annual allocations of the amount they are allowed to pollute (usually measured in tons). The allocation essentially represents a "right to pollute." Each company decides how to use its allowance. It can choose not to pollute (i.e., reduce emissions) by restricting output, switching to a cleaner fuel, or investing in scrubber technology. By not polluting, the company accumulates a surplus of credits which it can sell. Alternatively, the company can decide to pollute more than its allocation, and therefore be forced to purchase extra allowances on the open market.[19]

America's pollution market was widely seen as a success in curbing sulfur dioxide emissions and acid rain. When the United Nations turned to the problem of greenhouse gas emissions, cap and trade was one of the top candidates for a solution. The subsequent Kyoto Protocol, adopted in 1997 and ratified in 2005, not only set national carbon emission reduction targets, but it also set out a system of selling excess capacity to countries over their targets: a cap and trade system.

Opponents to cap and trade decry it as a morally bankrupt license to pollute. Criticism of the Kyoto Protocol's emissions markets in particular centered around the concept of "hot air," where countries can create carbon credits from actions that don't actually reduce emissions, such as curbing coal waste fires.[20]

As late as 2015, a report from the Stockholm Environment Institute found that 73% of Russia and Ukraine's offsets were for activities that would have happened anyway, such as wind farms that were built a decade ago—and therefore did not represent any meaningful form of emissions reduction.[21]

When a cap and trade on U.S. carbon emissions was brought to Congress in 2009 as the American Clean Energy and Security Act, NASA climate modeler James Hansen (one of the first scientists to alert the world of climate change risk) warned that a market-based approach restricts government's ability to regulate CO2 emissions, leads to "meager" emission reduction targets, and lacks controls over the trading of emission allowances.[22]

Even largely successful cap and trade markets draw criticism for their industry's perceived cynical use of their mechanisms. By the end of 2017 California's carbon market—described by some as the "best in the world"—had raised $6.5 billion for programs battling climate change and moved the state towards its ambitious target of achieving carbon emissions 40% below 1990 levels by 2030.

Yet in its May 2016 auction of emission allowances, only 11% of allowances offered were purchased; three months later, only one-third of its inventory was sold. By May the following year, it suffered a completely different problem. While every available allowance was sold at auction, observers feared companies were buying allowances to hoard—therefore doing nothing to reduce emissions.[23]

While well intended, the practical mechanism for offsetting carbon also added confusion and no small amount of cynicism to corporate claims of "being Green." Carbon offsets—or credits—are mechanisms for counterbalancing the carbon that businesses or individuals emit. The idea is that if you must emit CO2, then offsets provide a way to neutralize those emissions. Common offsetting programs include the creation of wind farms or the planting of forests.[24] When businesses or individuals engage in such offsetting projects, they earn certificates or credits as a way of balancing their own emissions. Yet the worth of such offset projects has often come into question.

The market for offsetting the carbon emitted from commercial flights is a case in point. Airline customers who want to offset the emissions of a commercial flight can buy offsets in online markets from a variety of providers. However, a 2008 report by The Guardian newspaper found that the measurement of the CO2 emitted for a flight from London Heathrow to New York JFK was calculated to be anywhere from 0.84 tons to 3.48 tons at a cost of between £8 to £69, depending on the carbon offsetting company used. The same report received quotes for a return trip from London to Sydney ranging from £9.48 to £643.39. When asked for their methodology, all carbon offsetting providers insisted they were measuring CO2 the same way. It was supposedly an apples-to-apples comparison with widely varying results.[25]

It is easy to see offsets and credits as akin to the "indulgences" sold by the Roman Catholic Church in the Middle Ages. As a form of penance for their sins, faithful Catholics of the time could buy so-called indulgences—monetary payments for absolution—from the church to avoid punishment in the afterlife. It was literally a way for the wealthy to buy their way out of purgatory.[26] Today, companies can "sin" by failing to meet emissions targets, then can claim to be free of their environmental sin in the form of offsets and credits. In reality, it is hard to argue that the purchase of offsets represents a legitimate change in the way they conduct business.

The issue with companies buying what are essentially a form of eco-indulgences is both moral and technical. The moral quandary is that like religious indulgences, buying offsets or credits is essentially buying salvation on their deathbed—rich companies buying the privilege of not needing to change their behavior or reduce their carbon footprint. The technical issue is that buying offsets or credits does not help a company accurately measure their carbon footprint. Instead, it encourages approximation of the carbon footprint, because by buying offsets, companies no longer need to measure their emissions comprehensively or consistently. Companies simply need to buy enough credits or offsets to cover their perceived liabilities.

Another technical issue with indulgences is how the offsets themselves are calculated. As we saw in the variability of carbon pricing for commercial flights, offset products are not always robust. Often, they are poorly or inconsistently measured, or they are hot air—they don't meaningfully reduce overall greenhouse gas emissions in any way.

Accurate measurement of an entity's carbon footprint is valuable information. It is material to a number of important metrics, such as energy and water usage. Yet even when companies try to accurately measure their carbon footprint, they often fail for lack of an appropriately robust metric.

Multiple studies have found that the methodologies used for measuring the carbon footprints consistently fall short of assessing true environmental impact. One 2012 study found that while retail giants such as Walmart, PepsiCo, and Tesco funded nonprofits to create their own measurement systems, the underlying science and data available at the time was not sufficient to provide an accurate impact of even the simplest of products, like paper.[27]

While methodologies have improved in the last eight years, corporate appetites for more accurate data might not have similarly improved.

How many large companies calculate their carbon footprint is often more of a guesstimate than an exercise in data-informed science. This can be especially true for multinationals with overseas holdings in developing countries, where utility suppliers cannot provide accurate consumption data. For these companies, calculation often involves using the data from one office—electricity bills, water usage, and waste—and extrapolating over the rest of the business. Not only is this an inaccurate way to measure a company's impact on the environment, but the information derived cannot meaningfully be utilized in any tactical or strategic way. Worse still, until recently, few companies included their suppliers in the calculation of their carbon footprint.

Is it any wonder the market is skeptical about the corporate carbon footprint claims?

The result of decades of cynical corporate advertising, hot air in emissions markets, inconsistencies in carbon offset pricing, and other greenwashing activities, is that the term "Green" has become indelibly linked with immeasurable claims. If anything can be Green, nothing is.

Greenwashing remains a problem even to this day, at every market level, from local residential real estate all the way to the global credit markets.

As late as 2018, a *Washington Post* investigation found that the residential real estate market was rife with greenwashing. Some local real estate agents and developers were found to be inflating a home's energy efficiency credentials or blatantly making false claims in a bid to ride the popularity of sustainable real estate.[28]

In March 2021, *Reuters* warned of greenwashing risks in global credit markets. Bonds linked to companies meeting certain environmental goals—so-called sustainability-linked bonds—were forecast to grow 20-fold to $150 billion in 2021 as businesses look to tap into booming demand. But the newswire warned that sustainability-linked bonds let companies raise money for general corporate purposes while only promising investors that if they do not meet sustainability targets, they will pay investors extra.[29] Such promises are largely untested in the market, *Reuters* warned, and the question remains how companies will measure—or duck—the meeting of potentially immeasurable goals.

The result of greenwashing and immeasurable claims is that Green initiatives are still (unfortunately) associated with downsides. When property developers talk about Green, it is often followed by a conversation about inflating budgets. When owners of older structures mention the need to modernize (code for sustainability), it is with a nod to the added expense they will incur.[30] The association between Green and downsides stemmed from both deliberate and unintended greenwashing, and was exacerbated by inadequate information on what it meant to be "Green" that was not backed by action.

The loophole needs to be closed on both the technical inability to measure carbon footprints, and the willful ignorance that some companies exhibit. For sustainability efforts to be transparent, an exacting form of measurement is required; otherwise, the real estate industry is at risk of a second wave of greenwashing. The last one set sustainability back decades. Society—and our planet—might not survive another delay.

Sustaining the Green movement

Sustainability was the natural next step in the evolution of Green. Where the Green movement was big on aspirations yet small on quantification, sustainability's argument was based on the age-old Return on Investment (ROI) formula: the real estate business is better off with lower risk and higher returns that sustainability provides.

Yet sustainability in its embryonic stage suffered from an overemphasis on "doing good" without the means to fully define what this good *was*—and why businesspeople should care beyond the basic tenet that "doing good is a good thing."

With shades similar to the evolution of Green, sustainability started as a general concept or philosophy for protecting the environment and natural resources. However, with a clear early focus on society's development and the built environment, sustainability was immediately more closely tied to real estate development.

In October 1987, the United Nations Commission on Environment and Development published the Brundtland Report as a 400-page treatise on the link between the environment and development, and the importance of thinking about the two together. It was the first time the term "sustainable development" was used, defined as "development that meets the needs of the present without compromising the ability of future generations to meet their own needs."[31]

The report was a turning point for the evolution of Green policies at every level of government. It was the impetus for increased global awareness of the need for action. It resulted in vast policy changes in the areas of energy, environmental protection, water usage, building zoning, air quality, and pollution (to name but a few). Eventually the report led to the UN's Sustainable Development Goals—a set of 17 global objectives for governments, business, and society to follow.

Alongside its goals to stimulate international cooperation at the governmental level, the UN sought to formulate "realistic action proposals" to deal with sustainable development and raise awareness while encouraging commitment from the business community.

Compared to the warm and fuzzy idea of Green-with-a-capital-G, sustainability was arguably a more targeted ethos. More so than Green, sustainability focused on the asset-level optimization of energy and carbon output. It provided a framework in which to understand how human activity impacted the environment, as well as direction—for individuals, corporates, governments, and the world—to solve the problem. Sustainability clarified the broad "How-Tos."

The UN's Sustainable Development Goals are a good example of sustainability's ability to supply a how-to framework. The interlinked goals are meant to be a global "blueprint to achieve a better and more sustainable future for all" by 2030.[32]

The World Green Building Council has identified nine of the UN's 17 goals as central to the real estate sector:[33]

Goal 3
Good health and wellbeing
Green buildings can improve people's health and wellbeing.

Goal 7
Affordable and clean energy
Green buildings can use renewable energy, becoming cheaper to run.

Goal 8
Decent work and economic growth
Building green infrastructure creates jobs and boosts the economy.

Goal 9
Industry innovation and infrastructure
Green building can spur innovation and contribute to climate resilient infrastructure.

Goal 11
Sustainable cities and communities
Green buildings are the fabric of sustainable communities and cities.

Goal 12
Responsible Consumption and Production
Green buildings use 'circular' principles, where resources aren't wasted.

Goal 13
Climate action
Green buildings produce fewer emissions, helping to combat climate change.

Goal 15
Life on land
Green buildings can improve biodiversity, save water resources and help protect forests.

Goal 17
Partnerships for the goals
Through building green we create strong, global partnerships.

However, to get from the Brundtland Report to a point where sustainability had a working definition—and then to practical guidelines for corporations—it took the better part of 30 years. The UN's Sustainable Development goals were not released until 2015. For decades, the exact definition of "Sustainable Development" was largely an academic debate of semantics and philosophy rather than practicality. A 1994 paper on the subject provides a pertinent example.[34] The author observes that no practical definition of sustainable development existed at the time: "If increasing the level of participation is a critical objective of SD, then a set of general criteria to guide the development of techniques... should be developed... Put differently, we need to say up to what point should a high weighting be accorded to adverse environmental effects."

The same paper submits that while the Brundtland formulation of sustainable development placed the linkage between environment and development at the top of the global agenda and stimulated discussion of sustainability, the concept of sustainable development was (in the mid 1990s) "plagued by a number of conceptual weaknesses and ambiguities" that reduced its ability to effect change.

Contrary to the claims of ratings, frameworks, and certification providers, sustainability has not until recently provided a uniform system for applying its principles in practice beyond the global or national level. And it has *never* supplied a detailed, actionable metric for measuring results for real estate projects or investment opportunities.

This failure was hardly the fault of the Brundtland Report, nor the various organizations that have since sought to implement its ambitious goals. The data simply wasn't granular enough for companies to track and monitor progress toward sustainability—at least not beyond the regional or national level.

Portfolio managers, market analysts, direct investors or even property owners would have found it difficult to quantify whether a property was "sustainable" or not, let alone the degree of its sustainability.

In the 1980s and 1990s, there was no easy way to ascertain sustainability data on a given investment opportunity. SEC-regulated companies could file paper copies of their financial statements up until the 1996 rollout of the watchdog's Electronic Data Gathering, Analysis, and Retrieval system (EDGAR). However, even though information contained in EDGAR is free and publicly available, there is still a significant delay between when companies file reports and when the public can access this documentation. Until 2000, companies filed reports on floppy disks which were then loaded into EDGAR by SEC staff.[35]

Quantifiable sustainability reporting did not exist until the mid 1990s and the creation of the Triple Bottom Line (TBL) framework—an accounting method for businesses to report social, environmental, and financial information. The three bottom lines are designed to measure a company's business operations in terms of (1) people, (2) planet, and (3) profit. Yet even the concept's creator, entrepreneur John Elkington, remarked in 2018 that TBL had been "reduced to a mere accounting tool, a way of balancing tradeoffs instead of actually doing things differently."[36]

Even in the present day, the practice "has not yet achieved full standardization and enforcement by the accounting standards setting organizations".[37] So, for real estate investors attempting to find actionable insight into investment opportunities, while TBL may have been helpful—assuming the target business was an early adopter of the new accounting method—it was not a reliable or comparable metric in its early years.

Stock indices tracking sustainable listed companies were a development of the late 1990s. The Dow Jones Sustainability Indices (DJSI) was launched in 1999 to track the success of publicly traded companies deemed sustainable. Equity indices are useful for identifying and tracking equity investments but do little for investors seeking private equity or direct real estate investment. It was not until 2017 that the first sustainable real estate index was launched. That year, Northern Trust Asset Management partnered with ESG performance monitor non-profit Global Real Estate Sustainability Benchmark (GRESB), to launch the Northern Trust GRESB Developed Real Estate ESG Index, which tracks the performance of developed market real estate investment trusts (REITs).[38]

In terms of awareness of the need for environmental considerations in business and investing, the concept of sustainability advanced society's understanding considerably. However, it has never in and of itself provided a framework for monitoring and measuring performance. Without a reliable and scalable way to measure and track sustainability at the asset level, the vast majority of market participants were unlikely to adopt the practice. This was especially true of the real estate sector.

Ask the average real estate developer in the '90s whether sustainability was important, and they would likely have told you that it was. However, they also would have remarked that it was too expensive to implement in practice. Various studies have shown a very convincing (and persistent) reason for this answer: Sustainability was just not the way things were done. As recently as 2017, researchers were blaming the failure of real estate developers to adopt sustainable development practices on a so-called rigidity trap identified by professionals in the industry: The "norms of practice within the real estate development industry combine with market and regulatory factors to favor existing practices and limit innovation."[39]

Up until only a few years ago, research suggested that real estate developers as a cohort decided that sustainable development was cost prohibitive. As a collective group, developers argued that sustainability was not worth the effort because of the increased upfront costs of Green materials, technologies, and certification fees, and the extra time it added to project schedules. After comparing the upfront costs to the vague benefits of doing good, they were not swayed by the argument.

Furthermore, these real estate professionals were not swayed by academic studies claiming sustainable development provides a market premium, and instead underestimated public demand. Says one researcher who has investigated this problem: "There is a general perception among private sector actors that sustainable urbanism is risky, which materializes as actual increased risk to developers because investors demand a quicker and higher rate of return for these projects."[40]

An emphasis on—and suspicion of—risk, explains researchers, is rooted in the industry's standard way of interpreting the market. Real estate investors typically use a precedent-based analysis method, where they examine five years of market performance of comparable properties to make valuations. But until recently, sustainable developments have traditionally lacked such comparable properties or sufficient data to complete this type of market analysis. For real estate professionals, the lack of data easily translates into a lack of trust in sustainable development practices, and alternative methods for valuation do not suffice.

For instance, one study found that market analysis evaluating a market's "willingness-to-pay" for hypothetical sustainable developments have had "less traction within the risk-adverse real estate industry because they are unproven prospects."[41]

From 1990 until (at least) the global financial crisis of 2008, developers who *did* try sustainable development were essentially doing so because they felt it was the right thing to do. They were not using data or market analysis to drive their decisions to go Green—in fact, they actively distrusted academic market analysis on sustainability and were making gut decisions rather than judgements backed by a scientific framework and metrics.[42]

None of this should be surprising. Real estate is a business. Market participants require reliable information to make their choices. Without such information on sustainability claims, buyers and sellers will default to using tried-and-true data to "go with what they know." That is why sustainability without robust measurement cannot convince pragmatic, profit-seeking market participants to go Green.

That is not to say today's asset owners are not serious about sustainability disclosure—especially when it is the law of the land. As is the case in many developed economies around the world, public companies in the United States have an obligation to disclose facts that are material to their business. In 2010, the SEC started requiring companies to disclose material, financial, and reputational risks associated with climate change. That same year, the International Organization for Standardization developed its ISO 26000 as guidelines for social responsibility reporting.[43]

The same laws that govern general and financial securities disclosures also govern sustainability disclosures. If a material fact is omitted from a company report: "a substantial likelihood that the disclosure of the omitted fact would have been viewed by the reasonable investor as having significantly altered the 'total mix' of the information made available." Which can be read as public companies that do not disclose sustainability information pertinent to their business are in breach of securities regulation.[44]

We will go into more detail on the role and requirements of regulated sustainability reporting in later chapters (particularly in Chapter 4), but it is worth making the point that sustainability reporting is limited when it comes to its usefulness for asset owners and investors. The most obvious limitation is that, depending on the jurisdiction, sustainability reporting is only done quarterly or annually. In a world where high-frequency traders rely on nanosecond trading advantages over their competition to beat the market, annual sustainability reports are not very useful for making fast investment decisions.

This is especially true of real estate companies, most of which in the U.S. are structured as REITs and traded daily on the stock exchange. Annual reports, by their nature, come out once a year. For 364 days of that year, their ability to provide actionable information is static.

The same logic applies to building operators and asset managers. If sustainability information is only gathered quarterly or annually for the purposes of regulatory reporting, the information is not useful to make tactical decisions in the day-to-day running of their operations.

There is also an issue of consistency of information. While the SEC requires companies to disclose sustainability information, it does not prescribe a specific format. As a result, a number of organizations have sought to provide reporting frameworks for filers to follow. The most prominent organizations in this space are the Carbon Disclosure Project (CDP), the Global Reporting Initiative (GRI), GRESB, and the Sustainability Accounting Standards Board (SASB). Some of these organizations are more focused on carbon emissions and environmental issues rather than social criteria. Some are global, while one (SASB) is purely U.S.-focused. Some provide a rating or scoring system, while others do not. Most provide reporting frameworks for both public and private companies, while only one (GRESB) provides a framework specifically for commercial real estate owners, asset managers, and developers.

A report can be significantly different depending on what reporting structure a company chooses to use. For this reason alone, the information compiled using one framework can be problematic to compare with information compiled using another framework. There is some fungibility, but it is by no means always apples-to-apples.

Let me be clear. I am not saying that the sustainability reports, ratings systems, frameworks, or metrics have no use whatsoever. Even in the 1990s and early 2000s, they were extremely innovative for their time. Such reporting and monitoring mechanisms not only help investors understand the basic differences between a sustainable and an unsustainable investment, but they also provide the foundation and taxonomy for more sophisticated and actionable metrics.

However, what sustainability reports, frameworks, or metrics do *not* provide is the data needed to drive the analysis required for benchmarking the market and providing timely, actionable information. These tools are a product of their times. The early metrics of the 1980s and 1990s were developed in a time when paper filings and floppy disks were the norm, when systems operated in isolation and did not share data easily. The reporting frameworks that emerged in the 2010s arose from a recognition of the increased importance of environmental regulatory compliance, but without any mechanism for addressing modern data reporting methods. These tools are essentially regulatory reporting frameworks, not tactical data feeds. And you can only probe so deep with regulatory information alone.

It has not been until the last few years that the data required for fast, tactical decision-making *and* deep analysis of an investment opportunity's health has even been available. But there was still one more step in the evolution of Green to come.

Making corporates socially responsible

In August 2019, a group of influential CEOs announced they were abandoning the long-held idea that the goal of corporations was to maximize profits for shareholders above all else. In their announcement, the Business Roundtable—an association of chief executives from around 200 of America's biggest companies—were leaning heavily on the principles of Corporate Social Responsibility (CSR) in their redefining of the *raison d'être* of companies.

"The American dream is alive, but fraying," Jamie Dimon, Chairman and CEO of JPMorgan Chase & Co. and Chairman of Business Roundtable, said in a statement introducing the 2019 Statement on the Purpose of a Corporation. "Major employers are investing in their workers and communities because they know it is the only way to be successful over the long term. These modernized principles reflect the business community's unwavering commitment to continue to push for an economy that serves all Americans."[45]

At the time of the announcement, America was in the throes of a national debate about the role corporations were playing in an increasingly inequitable society. Over the past few decades, workers' wages grew only modestly while chief executive compensation soared. Allegations abounded of businesses putting profits ahead of the needs of employees and customers—in areas including data privacy, healthcare, racial equality, and safety conditions.[46] In many ways, the Business Roundtable's Statement of Purpose was a recognition of the role of the private sector in shaping the fabric of society, and how corporate decisions impact communities in positive or negative ways.

Since its inception in 1972, the Business Roundtable had issued several Statements of Purpose over the years, all effectively emphasizing that profit for shareholders was a corporation's principal—if not sole— reason for existence. The 2019 statement was a marked change in attitude that signaled a true sea change in corporate mentality.

"This new statement better reflects the way corporations can and should operate today," added Alex Gorsky, Chairman of the Board and Chief Executive Officer of Johnson & Johnson and Chair of the Business Roundtable Corporate Governance Committee. "It affirms the essential role corporations can play in improving our society when CEOs are truly committed to meeting the needs of all stakeholders."

CSR is a framework for self-regulating a business so that it can maximize its positive impacts on the environment and society.[47] The concept has been traced back to at least the late 1800s, when concerns over the societal impact of the Industrial Revolution permeated from the long hours and poor conditions to which factory workers were subjected at the time.

In its modern conception, CSR is mostly a product of the Twentieth Century. In the 1950s, business owners started thinking more seriously about their overall responsibility and involvement in the community in which they lived and worked. By the late 1960s, companies started focusing on specific issues like pollution, racial discrimination, and urban decay. And in the 1970s, companies began responding to these problems by creating management, organizational, and operational actions to address environmental and societal issues.[48]

Two notable examples that continue to this day are the Body Shop, founded in the UK in 1976 and Ben & Jerry's, founded in 1978. These two companies put CSR front and center in their business strategies.

The Body Shop began its Trade Not Aid program in 1987, with a commitment to sourcing ethical ingredients and accessories from thousands of producers around the globe. It has contributed substantially to the economic wellbeing of many communities in the developing world. For instance, in Ghana, 640 women from 11 villages handcraft the company's shea butter using traditional techniques passed down through generations. The business provides an independent income for the women, and the Body Shop pays a premium price to help fund community projects that it says positively impact the lives of 49,000 people across 11 villages in the region, including the building of seven schools that educate around 1,200 students every year, and access to safe water and healthcare facilities.[49]

When Ben & Jerry's was founded in 1978, its founders penned a three-part mission statement: make the world's best ice cream, run a financially successful company, and "make the world a better place." In pursuit of that mission, over the years the company sourced from regional organic dairy farms, only used milk free of artificial growth hormones, and made fair-trade and organic ingredients priorities. When the company was sold to multinational Unilever it ensured provision in the acquisition that the company would still operate in the same manner, and that the founders could still use the Ben & Jerry's platform for their ESG priorities.[50]

Yet the idea also had its detractors. Nobel Prize-winning economist Milton Friedman famously rejected the idea of a corporate social responsibility in 1970 as "pure and unadulterated socialism,"[51] eventually coining the mantra the "business of business is business."

Perhaps partially in response to Friedman, in 1971 the Committee for Economic Development adapted age-old theories of the 'social contract' to businesses. Companies function and exist, the theory goes, because of public consent. They are therefore obligated to contribute to the needs of society.

Since then, the market has become even more convinced of the importance of corporate goals beyond simply profit maximization. By 2015, 92% of the world's largest companies in the world produced CSR reports and Fortune Global 500 firms spent approximately $20 billion annually on CSR activities.[52]

CSR acquired new resonance in the mid-2000s, during the expansion of globalization and international trade.[53] Businesses were becoming more complex and demands for enhanced transparency and improved corporate citizenship swelled, all while global economies dealt with the global financial crisis of 2007-2008. However, even before the financial crisis, notable experts such as Harvard economist Michael Porter were calling CSR an "inescapable priority for business" as "governments, activists, and the media have become adept at holding companies to account for the social consequences of their activities."[54]

Like sustainability statements, corporate social responsibility reports are now a mainstay of company communications. Combined, they can provide companies with a clear purpose that can be communicated to all stakeholders.

However, several studies show that even the most seemingly positive CSR goals can become negatives for companies if they are perceived to be cynical or poorly executed.

A 2017 experiment found that when employees suspected their employer was using CSR initiatives purely to achieve economic benefits for themselves, the employees reacted negatively and put in less effort. "In other words," observed the researchers, "while these initiatives will benefit society, they will backfire for companies if people think they're being used for the wrong reasons."[55]

The same benefits of sustainability are generally ascribed to CSR. Socially responsible companies improve the communities in which they operate and reduce their impact on the environment. For businesses themselves, properly executed CSR policies should help companies mitigate various risks (such as climate, reputational, and legal), differentiate their brand, provide a competitive advantage, and ensure compliance to the regulations of the jurisdictions in which they operate.

If CSR has a central failing, it may be its subjectivity. Definitions of what is socially responsible (AKA good) beyond the most general terms are often idiosyncratic. Absent a consensus definition, business leaders are left to their own devices to decide what constitutes being socially responsible. Yet even if there was a consensus, what is good practice for one organization might not be good practice for another. And that's not necessarily a bad thing. Businesses are not monoliths. They sell different products and serve different communities. It is understandable that they will articulate CSR in different ways. Yet the subjective nature of CSR means it does not offer objective strategies for improving a given problem.

Ultimately, what is good is what all stakeholders—employees, management, shareholders, and customers—agree works for them. What is more important, from a business management and monitoring perspective, is whether activities are clear and transparent. For the purposes of tactical or strategic moves, CSR reports on their own hold little in the way of such information. CSR reports cannot inform executives how to run their companies—how to specifically allocate value, money, time, or energy. CSR compliance measurements often use nonsystematic frameworks, questionnaire-based surveys, or other approximate measures of undefined goals.

As a result, CSR reports do not provide the granular measurement and monitoring necessary to make business decisions. They are essentially a framework for doing good, not step-by-step directions or the systematic measuring of a company's performance. What is necessary to run a company—including real estate companies—is evidence of progress towards empirically defined goals and the resulting quantifiable outcomes. As worthy as CSR is, it does not provide such measurement or information. Instead, it must rely on a more scientific tool. Enter ESG.

ESG: The fulfillment of a promise

The concept of ESG—that environmental, social, and corporate governance issues can impact a company's health and performance—has been around for decades. But it was not until a 2005 conference organized by the World Bank's International Finance Corporation (IFC) that there was any true consensus around its definition. In a report endorsed by 20 financial institutions with combined assets under management of over $6 trillion, the IFC developed guidelines and recommendations on how to better integrate ESG issues into investing.

As an example of ESG factors which impact a company's health, the consortium provided the following:[56]

Environmental issues:

- ➤ Mitigate climate change and related risks
- ➤ Reduce toxic releases and waste
- ➤ Develop new regulation expanding environmental liability
- ➤ Meet the needs of society to improve performance, transparency and accountability, leading to reputational risks if not managed properly
- ➤ Create markets for environmental services and environment-friendly products

Social issues:

- ➤ Improve workplace health and safety
- ➤ Improve community relations
- ➤ Address human rights issues at company and supplier/contractor premises
- ➤ Foster improvement in government and community relations in operations in developing countries
- ➤ Meet the needs of society to improve performance, transparency, and accountability, leading to reputational risks if not managed properly

Corporate governance issues:

- ➤ Refine board structures and accountability
- ➤ Practice better accounting and disclosure
- ➤ Improve audit committee structure and the independence of auditors
- ➤ Align executive compensation with values and expectations of a more equitable society
- ➤ Better manage corruption and bribery issues

That same year, the UN's Environment Program Finance Initiative (UNEP FI) asked law firm Freshfields Bruckhaus Deringer to investigate the legal foundation for investors to use ESG criteria in their decision-making. Freshfields concluded that not only was it permissible, but that financial analysts and institutional investment decision-makers also arguably had a fiduciary duty to include such due diligence in their investment analysis.[57]

Since then, the use of ESG criteria has become ubiquitous. The Organization for Economic Co-operation and Development (OECD) estimates that the combined value of professionally-managed portfolios with ESG assessments exceeds $17.5 trillion globally, with the growth of ESG-related traded investment vehicles exceeding $1 trillion.[58] The methods for measuring ESG criteria have become more sophisticated since 2005 as well. In a 2019 whitepaper, asset manager BlackRock estimated there were now over 1,000 indices devoted to ESG, while market data companies that provide ESG ratings include Bloomberg, Morningstar, S&P, Thomson Reuters, and MSCI.

Green, sustainability, SRI, and ESG investing all follow two basic styles: **avoid** and **advance**. Avoidance is staying away from investments that pose certain risks (like oil companies) or violate the investor's values (like tobacco and firearms). Advancing is finding companies that meet the investor's values (like solar energy providers) and sustainability criteria (like Green buildings). The difference between ESG and the preceding forms of values-based investing is that ESG provides an extra layer of probity and more granular information on an asset. It is better at identifying and rating specific risks. It is "intended to bring new insights to investment through new sources of data."[59]

ESG is the defense against greenwashing and the fulfillment of the promises embedded in sustainability. It is a way to move beyond the old misconceptions and prejudices that came from the basic concept of Green. ESG differs from Green-with-a-capital-G, sustainability, and even CSR, because it presents a method for being prescriptive about the data and measures used to support the concept's premise. With its environmental, social, and governance components, ESG is also a more inclusive concept that moves beyond the limits of "Green" and CSR.

The evolution from Green aspirations to quantifiable ESG benchmarks has profound implications for the real estate industry. The message of Green was: *Be transparent about your business.* ESG asks: *"Can you measure the totality of your business and report it?"* The step from general sustainability frameworks to ESG metrics represents a maturation of business practices to a more precise measurement of a portfolio's performance. In 2022, we now find ourselves at a point in the evolution from Green to ESG because of a convergence of three phenomena: The **data is here**, the **technology is here**, and the **market wants it**.

The data is here

There are now multiple sources of data that can be used in the measuring of a building's ESG performance.

Energy usage, carbon emissions, water usage, and waste disposal all cost money. Because of this, utility companies keenly track their customers' usage and expenditure. Building maintenance often requires copious account-keeping and procurement protocols to ensure a building is operating effectively and efficiently.

The use of electricity, water, and waste also all now have comprehensive regulatory frameworks where building owners must report on their carbon emissions, and water usage to their municipalities, state, or national governments. Additionally, if a property owner wants their building certified Green, there is a plethora of information they must provide. Even if they do not wish to "go Green" for ethical reasons, real estate developers and owners increasingly face stricter governance requirements from their boards, stockholders, and various other stakeholders—including their customers. Not only do these stakeholders require documentary evidence of an asset's sustainability, a real estate company's activities— board decisions, stock price, building sales prices and leases—are data points in and of themselves.

Utility bills, maintenance expenditure, regulatory compliance, certification frameworks, sales figures, and lease terms; at every point in a building's life cycle, data and information is created.

For investment decision-makers, there is arguably already a superabundance of data.[60] Data aggregators provide extensive sets of data pulled from public sources. Ratings agencies offer a composite view that lets investors compare opportunities. Specialist data firms concentrate on specific ESG criteria or industry sectors. Machine learning and artificial intelligence is providing increasingly new and innovative ways to both find and analyze this data.

The technology is here

A lot of the technology required to make a building sustainable already exists today and has for a long time. Energy efficient light bulbs, solar energy, low flow plumbing fixtures, ENERGY STAR appliances, and building optimization systems have been around for decades. All these building technologies have the ability to collect usage data. What has been missing until recently is a way to derive and unite data from these disparate technologies.

As a result of the increased availability of data from building technologies and third-party suppliers, there are now technologies for monitoring and reporting almost everything in real estate: energy management, building maintenance schedules, bill management, carbon monitoring, Green certification, regulatory reporting, and investor communications.

Yet previously these systems could not easily talk to each other. Until the advent of big data and Application Programming Interfaces (APIs), it was common for companies to, for example, take their energy usage information, paste it into a spreadsheet to provide to the financial regulator, then paste it into *another* format to publish as part of their corporate social responsibility report on their website. The information was difficult to retrieve and collate—and it was a manual task. Measuring, managing, and disclosing ESG data is not easy when it cannot be combined into a unified reporting system.

The act of adequately measuring ESG criteria requires extracting a vast quantity of disparate data from extremely varied sources. Lease accounting systems contain information about the number of properties owned, how big those properties are, where they're located, and their occupancy rates. Data on resource usage comes from the utilities companies that sell energy and water to buildings. Other necessary inputs are regulation compliance status, Green certifications, and project data on how buildings are implementing improvements.

All this data needs to be quality assured and analyzed. If a company does not have adequate quality assurance of its data, the data it reports is not credible. The more a company knows, the higher its confidence level in its reporting, and the better it is able to use that knowledge to make informed decisions about its operations.

To interrogate ESG data, it also needs to be standardized so that users can compare the data from one building or investment with another. For data to be useful, it needs to move beyond a place where the information gathered is subjective—where it is a matter of opinion—to a place where it can be quantified.

In the real estate ecosystem, the consumers of a company's data—the building managers, shareholders, regulators, certifiers, and clients—all need objective, quantifiable data. Regulators need reliable information to assess compliance. Shareholders, investors, ratings agencies, and lenders all require robust data to better understand the health of a company. Prospective buyers or lessors need transparent information to compare properties. Data located on disparate spreadsheets, communicated ad hoc in a phone call, or backed up by a generic Green certification is not objective, quantifiable data for the purposes of benchmarking or making specific decisions.

As the real estate industry becomes more sophisticated in its desire to use sustainability information to make decisions, it needs to improve the way it collects and tracks metrics. ESG provides that.

ESG metrics can pinpoint information about an asset and provide actionable insight which can be used to make tactical and strategic decisions. Systems which monitor energy consumption and water usage can be used to identify inefficiencies and provide an opportunity for improvement. For instance, with the advent of the Internet of Things (IoT), internet-connected sensors can feed energy usage data from air conditioners and other large household appliances into a building maintenance system, adding a deeper understanding of the company's energy usage. Smart sprinkler monitors that identify leaks not only improve building safety but can also be used to manage water usage and plan maintenance and repair schedules.

The market increasingly wants ESG information

The real estate industry has reached a point where decisions to become sustainable are based on a tacit agreement that the move has a positive impact on revenue, reduces operating costs and capitalization rates, and leads to higher property values. Not everyone thinks this way (yet), but it is a growing trend based on contemporary consensus.

When I was a real estate broker, I saw examples of sustainable practices every day—from energy efficiency to improved tenancy engagement— that consistently led to an asset's outperformance. Real estate professionals know implicitly that when operating expenses decrease, net operating income of a building improves. However, as a broker I was initially surprised to see that in terms of winning financing— obtaining institutional investors to commit money to an asset—there was a causal link between good sustainability practices and lower costs of capital, such as preferred interest rates on the debt or better underwriting criteria.

Part of the explanation for this causality is that institutional investors do not usually buy real estate at the asset level. Instead, they buy assets at the fund level. And at the fund level, ESG, CSR, and sustainability criteria are an important part of the institutional investors' due diligence process. The causal link between asset price premiums and ESG metrics becomes obvious when you consider that asset prices are heavily influenced by the due diligence processes—and underlying principles—used by institutional market participants.

ESG is material to the real estate business when it helps people make money. And there is a lot of evidence that there is indeed a premium for greener buildings. Rental performance and the sale price of a property has been proven to be positively improved by the greenness of a building. Academic studies unearthed this insight around a decade ago.

One study found a rental premium of around 6% for LEED and ENERGY STAR certification, as well as a sale price premium of 35% for LEED rated buildings and 31% for ENERGY STAR rated buildings.[61] Since then, pension funds, sovereign wealth funds, and other long-term investors who put tens of billions of dollars into real estate have found that strong ESG metrics are not just a proxy for better returns, but also for improved risk mitigation.

Institutional investors, such as university endowments and sovereign wealth funds, hate risk and love returns. It is for this reason that they expect accurate ESG information from their investments and expect asset owners to strive towards improving the greenness of their operations. Otherwise, these big pools of capital will increasingly choose not to do business with a given company that cannot prove their ESG credentials.

As ESG metrics are progressively adopted by institutional investors, their use by real estate companies becomes even more existential than a specific building being sold for a slightly higher or lower price, depending on its Green credentials. Instead, ESG becomes the lifeblood of the entire real estate industry. If a company cannot obtain access to capital, it will cease to exist.

To use a gambling analogy, ESG is becoming table stakes. It is the price of admission. If real estate companies do not find ways to accurately measure ESG, they will relinquish their ability to participate in the market, or to even play the game. However, the better real estate companies are at ESG, the higher will be their competitive advantage, leading to more access to capital, better economic returns, and less risk.

It should be mentioned that the clarion call to ESG is not necessarily for the construction industry—especially in the developed world. Regulations in the U.S. and Europe are now mature and sophisticated enough that developers have heeded the message. Generally, developers now use modern building products and designs which are state-of-the-art in terms of their sustainability. Newly built assets are not the energy-inefficient underperformers that they were in previous decades. Developers are creating healthy spaces for their occupiers.

The bulk of the ESG challenge lies with existing buildings. Yet many owners simply do not comprehend that they have a problem. They are unaware that their buildings are consuming far more energy and water than they need to, and that they are creating unhealthy environments for occupiers. When asset owners are made aware of unnecessary drains on their operating costs, they are always motivated to improve. After all, a real estate owner's entire business is maximizing profit from their buildings. ESG metrics provide that motivation—and tell operators *how* to improve their operations.

Perhaps for this reason above all others, the real estate industry needs to better utilize high-quality data. It needs to understand what ESG means and how to measure it in a consistent way—from building to building, market to market, and globally. ESG data needs to be the same caliber of information as traditional financial data, because if the data is not of a high and consistent quality, then real estate market participants understandably will not trust it—and it will sound, once more, like greenwashing.

The good news is that the data is there. And it is improving. It just needs to be adopted more widely.

ESG presents an opportunity for real estate owners to find new levers to create greater value. Until now, the real estate industry has been able to find and create value through only a narrow set of tools: property leasing or principal appreciation. ESG creates a new set of tools for the real estate entity to create value through governance. Using ESG metrics, a real estate entity can reduce its impact on the environment and, as a result, obtain credit for its actions through better access to capital.

Real estate professionals need to understand that ESG is not an anchor. It is a balloon.

Chapter 2:
"E" Means Existential

In 2013, I had just launched a company called Measurabl into the white space that was ESG software for the real estate sector. One of the first people I visited after starting my company was Vance Maddocks, President of CBRE Global Investors' flagship U.S. office investment platform, Strategic Partners. Vance had started at CBRE in 1984. He became the firm's President of Americas not long thereafter. Vance was known as a forward thinking, consummate real estate professional.

I told Vance about my new company, our technology vision (yet to be turned into any actual code) and asked him how much he thought ESG data would be worth to fund managers who invest in real estate. After all, if I could not confirm there was any meaningful appetite to spend on sustainability technology, my business would need a quick recalibration. I'll never forget what Vance said:

"Well, Matt, let me put it this way: I can do 'sustainability', and continue to draw investor interest in our fund or I can risk ceding those dollars to my competitors. The cost of that risk is in the billions to me. You can figure out the fee from there."

When Vance made this remark, it was the first time that I truly understood the power of investor pressure on a fund manager—and the impact it can have on the flow of capital.

Yet this was already a view that was beginning to take hold in the investment community. By 2012, the number of climate and environmental shareholder resolutions had increased from 10 in 1999 to 109. Threatening to pull their capital, shareholders convinced Avon, Hershey, and Smucker's to source 100% certified sustainable palm oil. In 2013, shareholders forced Continental Resources to end the wasteful burning of natural gas in the Bakken region of North Dakota.[1]

A few months later, I was driving through Colorado when I received a panicked call from the head of real estate at a big investment bank.

"You were referred to me by one of your customers," he said with no small hint of urgency. "How fast can you put your service to work?"

I told him I was driving through the Rockies and asked if he would not mind waiting until I made it through the pass. But he was adamant.

"I have my executive team circled up. All we need to know is when you can start and what the cost is."

It turned out he had just received a visit from one of his most important investors. They were considering pulling their money if they did not start at minimum measuring and reporting on ESG.

I have since had hundreds of these calls. Although the urgency and focus may vary, the same basic drivers—investor pressure, regulation, and customer (tenant) preferences—were omnipresent.

When it came to investor sentiment towards sustainability, Vance turned out to be a canary in the coal mine. Less than two years later, a slew of major investors in real estate began insisting that their investment measure and disclose ESG performance, or these investors would divest from their funds.

ESG has become crucial, even existential, for institutional real estate investors looking to raise money for their funds.

An investor-driven market

There was a time in the not-so-distant past that most retail financial advisors would reject ESG funds outright. Their argument was that their job was to make money for their clients by finding investments that would maximize returns. In fact, they had a duty to find the highest-performing funds. By taking ESG into consideration, they argued, financial advisors would be neglecting their fiduciary duty. Therefore, they would not recommend ESG investments to their clients.[2] Some financial advisors still think this way. But they are a dying breed.

In 2017, a Bank of America Merrill Lynch—now BofA Securities—study claimed that when investors selected stocks in the top 20% of ESG rankings, they suffered less price volatility and lower price declines. In addition, if investors only held companies in their portfolios with above-average environmental and social scores, they would have avoided most of the company bankruptcies that occurred within the five-year period of the study. Of those findings, a research group from the UNEP Finance Initiative said:

"These results appear to statistically validate the value proposition of investing in the stock of companies with superior ESG profiles, as measured by equity valuations. Similarly, the results demonstrate that ESG integration is an effective risk mitigation technique, as companies that rank higher on ESG attributes historically have exhibited lower risks based on price and earnings volatility (and even bankruptcy risk) compared to their lower-ranked peers."[3]

By 2018, 90% of investors believed that ESG portfolios performed as well or better than non-ESG portfolios, according to a study by the Royal Bank of Canada.[4] A recent study from ratings agency Morningstar revealed that over the last decade, almost 60% of ESG funds won investors higher returns than equivalent non-ESG funds.[5]

In the investment world, data matters. And it drives decision-making.

How institutional investors think about ESG

Heitman is a 55-year-old real estate investment firm with $43.4 billion in assets under management. In 2016 the firm hired Laura Craft to manage ESG across their global portfolio. Before joining Heitman, Craft had spent a decade managing ESG at the $59 billion AUM LaSalle Investment Management. In the last 15 years, Craft has evaluated the sustainability of thousands of real estate assets based on strict ESG metrics and has a keen understanding of how institutional investors use ESG to make decisions.

Front of mind for Craft—whether she is looking to provide credit to building owners, entering a joint-venture, or investing in a listed REIT—is the "G" in ESG: Governance.

"Our number one concern is the core governance structure of the company. Companies that score higher on governance have typically lower cost of capital and are better run companies. They also tend to have better environmental and social programs," Craft says. "There is a greater link of correlation and value with higher governance scores. Top of mind is that the company we are lending to or investing in will have in place similar ESG guidelines and policies to our own."

Heitman is one of a growing number of large institutional real estate investment firms that over time have moved ESG to the center of their decision-making process. The shift in strategy might seem revolutionary for a traditional firm founded 55 years ago, but Craft says the transformation is not only a natural evolution of investment practices, it is essential to evaluating risk and reward on any major investment. The reason, says Craft, is simply because ESG considerations impact value. And value is what drives the long-term real estate market.

"In the 1990s, real estate investing was about the art of the deal. Investors became experts in reading and modeling financial statements to determine value and get an edge over the competition. Yet in the early 2000s there was a flattening of financial information—everyone had the same data," explains Craft. "To differentiate and better model an investment's potential, institutional investors had to think about things their competitors did not have. ESG data was one of those areas. As non-financial data became more available, ESG rose in importance as something that could be modeled to help make sound business decisions."

Craft considers ESG principles as now part of Heitman's DNA, impacting decision-making across the investment house.

"It is not a siloed department. For our private equity investments, our entire acquisition team—the ones finding properties for us—use it in their analysis. Our asset managers use it to manage our properties. It is baked into our entire operations throughout the stages of the investment lifecycle," Craft says.

From rewarding good behavior to punishing bad

Momentum slowly gained ground for ESG as a positive measure that should be rewarded by investors. However, in January 2020 the negatives of ignoring ESG and sustainability came into full view. Suddenly, ignoring ESG would be punished by the markets.

The warning came in BlackRock CEO Larry Fink's now-famous 2020 letter to CEOs, informing them of how the heavyweight investment firm would choose companies to invest in. For Fink, corporate survival and sustainability were causal: "A company's prospects for growth are inextricable from its ability to operate sustainably... Actions that damage society will catch up with a company and destroy shareholder value."

Fink warned CEOs who desire capital injections from the biggest asset manager on the planet that they *would not be financed* if they did not include ESG and sustainability in their business strategies. The $7.43 trillion AUM manager now requires the companies in which it invests to provide disclosure consistent with the Sustainability Accounting Standards Board and the Task Force on Climate-related Financial Disclosures (TCFD). Fink said BlackRock would "vote against management and board directors when companies are not making sufficient progress on sustainability-related disclosures".

When the global Coronavirus pandemic hit a few months later, many commentators and market participants were expecting attention to be diverted from climate. However, the market's response was precisely the opposite. That year saw a flight by investors to ESG funds as the market sought safer harbors in a time of extreme volatility. By the second quarter, assets under management in ESG index funds hit $250 billion—20% of the total market. In Europe, assets had quadrupled since 2016.[6] By November 2020, mutual fund and Exchange-Traded Fund (ETF) investors put $288 billion in sustainable assets—a 96% increase over 2019.[7] JPMorgan Chase estimated in early 2021 that globally around $7.2 trillion was invested using ESG guidelines, up from $3 trillion the year prior, with 80% of that money invested in Europe.[8]

As we saw in Chapter 1, sophisticated investors—including pension funds, sovereign wealth funds, and hedge funds—long held that ESG metrics helped them find successful investments. Investors such as BlackRock and Blackstone, and pension funds such as Dutch PGGM and Californian CalPERS are increasingly choosing to invest or divest based on ESG factors. Blackstone, with $619 billion under management, uses an evaluation of ESG considerations in its pre- and post-investment decision making as "a standard part of the investment and the asset/portfolio management processes" for every investment, whether or not it is in the firm's ESG-labeled funds.[9] Dutch pension fund PGGM, which manages around €266 billion, uses SASB's Materiality Map to provide "consistent assessment" of individual ESG factors in the sectors and investments it considers.[10] By 2022, the $444 billion California Public Employees' Retirement System (CalPERS) plans to integrate ESG factors into all its investment decisions.[11]

The retail market caught up with institutional investors by 2020. More individuals were using ESG to influence their investments than ever before. Fink attributes much of this shift to the improved metrics and evaluation tools that are now available to a wider set of investors.

"Not long ago, building a climate-aware portfolio was a painstaking process, available only to the largest investors," Fink wrote in a letter to CEOs early 2021. "Better technology and data are enabling asset managers to offer customized index portfolios to a much broader group of people."[12]

Two further developments contributed to opening the market to a wider range of investors: The establishment of exchange-traded funds (ETFs) and the broadening in the United States of who can invest in sophisticated investment vehicles.

The rise of the ETF

Exchange-traded funds have seen a boon of retail capital in the past decade. As the name suggests, ETFs are investment vehicles arranged as funds composed of stocks, bonds, commodities, derivatives, and a whole host of other assets—including physical properties such as residential complexes, office buildings, factories, or entire real estate portfolios. Unlike mutual funds—the main constituent of 401(k)s and pension funds—ETFs are listed and traded on the stock exchange. Public trading brings the promise of liquidity, but it also brings a higher level of regulatory oversight, and the governance of ETFs must be as robust as that of other listed companies.

ETFs emerged from the popularity of index funds during the 1980s and '90s as a way to passively invest in the markets without having to do the work of selecting individual stocks. By 2005, total market capitalization of the vehicles was around $281 million,[13] but by the end of 2020 the amount of money invested in ETFs topped $5 trillion.[14]

If there is a market for a product or commodity, it can generally be wrapped in an ETF. Country-based ETFs buy specific indices to let people invest in a specific geography—such as Germany, Europe, or the world. Some ETFs invest solely in one commodity, such as precious metals or agricultural commodities. Often marketed as "themed" investments—growth funds, value funds, sector funds—the list of ETF compositions is seemingly endless. All the biggest and most popular fund managers and 401(k) providers offer real estate-specific ETFs—Vanguard, iShares, Schwab, Fidelity, JP Morgan, Invesco—most 401(k)s and pensions would now have at least one real estate ETF in their composition.

The latest development in the ETF market is ESG-themed ETFs that invest along a variety of sustainability goals. So-called ESG ETFs have recently seen a boom in popularity. The market grew 223% growth year-over-year in 2020 and reached a record capitalization of $189 billion—largely from $97 billion in net inflows and almost 200 new ESG ETFs launching on the market that year.[15]

The availability of these easy-to-find investment opportunities cannot be underestimated as a significant contributor to the growth in the average citizen's awareness of ESG. Accessibility strengthened the appetite of the average person / casual investor for sustainable investments. And the knock-on effect of greater demand is a greater imperative to offer such funds. From that flows pressure on the underlying assets—the companies and properties within the funds—to meet higher ESG standards. This virtuous cycle is set to continue.

A greater interest among investors

Another recent development in the U.S. that is set to raise the popularity of sustainable investments—especially in real estate—is modifications to the SEC's definition of who is a sophisticated investor. In America, there are legal restrictions on who can invest in certain types of sophisticated or complex investments—such as hedge funds, private equity, and certain complex derivatives that are not registered with the SEC. The financial watchdog's rationale for the prohibitions is to protect the average citizen (who is deemed to have little knowledge of investments) from losing their savings on bets they do not understand.

Only "accredited investors" that meet the SEC's definition are permitted to invest in complex investment vehicles. Companies offering such investments are prohibited from marketing or selling to non-accredited investors. The definition of who qualifies as an accredited investor has remained largely unchanged for decades: Individuals with an annual income of $200,000 (or $300,000 for couples) or a net worth in over $1 million (excluding the family home). In late 2020 the SEC expanded the definition to include, among other criteria, new categories for people who can demonstrate their understanding of investing and the ability for non-married couples to pool assets to qualify. Such adjustments may seem technical and small in scope, but they have the potential to considerably expand the pool of people who can invest in non-listed real estate vehicles, hedge funds, impact investing funds, and a host of other capital-raising instruments.

A significant influx of fresh capital, combined with a greater focus on sustainable investments, will likely have a knock-on effect in the institutional market and will result in new models of direct investment in sustainable real estate and other Green investment products.

ESG brings a premium—if you have the data to prove it

Real world examples abound of commercial real estate companies using ESG data to attract more investors at a premium.

Frankfurt-listed real estate investment company Corestate Capital builds and manages funds and other investment vehicles for institutional investors, high net worth families, and private investors. It offers private investments and fund management in both equity and debt across a variety of asset types, including residential, offices, industrial properties, hospitality, and retail spaces. By 2020, the firm managed €28 billion and had 70,000 in retail clients with a mandate to find and manage sustainable and profitable investment solutions based on ESG principles.[16]

Corestate credits much of its success to its ability to digitally monitor and analyze ESG data from the hundreds of properties it owns or provides credit for at any one time. However, when the firm first embarked on offering sustainable real estate, the team quickly realized that investors needed more than just a promise and good intentions.

Once it was able to start measuring its ESG performance, Corestate was able to go building by building and across its portfolios to identify areas where it could improve performance. By 2019 it was able to use ESG metrics to show investors a 12% reduction in CO_2 emissions over the previous year and achieve a 10% reduction in energy use in a single year.

New York-based private equity firm GTIS Partners felt tracking and visualizing ESG data over its $4.4 billion portfolio was crucial to keeping and attracting new capital.

GTIS has established a strong reputation in the real estate space—in 2019 its GTIS Brazil Real Estate Fund was recognized by GRESB for the fifth consecutive year as the most sustainable private equity real estate fund in South America. More recently, for the company's U.S. portfolio, GTIS digitized the process of collection, analysis, and reporting of ESG data, with positive results.

"This is a new age where we're starting to think about ESG data almost as if it were financial data," says Hal Doueck, former Vice President, Real Estate Private Equity at GTIS. "Analysis of this data, along with its associated risks and opportunities, empowers us to enhance the long-term sustainable performance of our portfolios."[17]

Better data capture and analysis helped GTIS's funds improve sustainability performance.

"In many ways, ESG is the new frontier of investing, both because investors expect it and because it makes good business sense. For years now, we've pushed ourselves to meet a higher threshold of expectations in our Brazil real estate investing activities by thinking of tomorrow, not just today," says Josh Pristaw, GTIS's Head of Capital Markets and Co-head of Brazil. "To accomplish this, we recalibrated our models to put sustainability criteria at the heart of our investment process."[18]

In January 2021, Hong Kong developer New World Development became the first real estate developer to offer a U.S.-Dollar sustainability-linked bond. The company wished to raise $200 million, and they were over-scribed by a multiple of six with investors wanting to fund them. New World linked the fundraising with a promise to achieve 100% renewable energy for all its Guangdong-Hong Kong-Macau Greater Bay Area rental properties by 2026.[19]

A year earlier, the storied Montage Beverly Hills hotel sold for a record per-room price for a Beverly Hills property.[20] The sellers—Ohana Real Estate Investors—reengineered the property to reduce energy consumption by 8% with a lifetime carbon reduction of 1,789 tons. Ohana, which focuses on the luxury hospitality sector, said at the time that the increased net operating income that came from its sustainability efforts was "value-additive" to the sale.[21]

These examples underline a crucial point about the mindset of the investor, who is now more focused on an investment opportunity's potential risk versus reward. Investors want returns, but they want them adjusted for risk. ESG has been adopted by the market as a strong empirical set of criteria for evaluating and mitigating risk. It helps investors determine if they are lowering their risk, and therefore find superior risk-adjusted returns.

What investors are looking for in an ESG-principled real estate investment obviously differs from investor to investor. Most are looking for properties that can prove they consider their environmental impact in some way or another. At the very least, they want lower carbon emissions and high energy efficiency. For obvious reasons, effective governance is also high on the list for most investors—especially pension funds, endowments, and sovereign wealth funds, which need to answer to their shareholders and other stakeholders.

Societal factors are also holding increasing importance to investors. The rise of the 'S' in ESG predates the events of 2020, however the global coronavirus pandemic further raised societal concerns around things such as healthy air and clean spaces. The Black Lives Matter movement shone a harsh spotlight on pervasive inequality concerns, such as access to quality housing. How firms measure 'E,' 'S,' and 'G' has become a critical issue for investors. If they are to enjoy access to capital, asset owners need to be able to not only prove their credentials to the market. They also must have the data to explain any failings and present plans for improvement.

What investors want: Environmental

Institutional and retail investors alike want to know whether their real estate asset managers are adequately managing and mitigating the risks of climate change. They require information about their properties' carbon footprint and energy efficiency statistics: How much energy is burned from fossil fuels versus alternative energy sources? How much water is being used by the building and is it taking steps to optimize water usage? Investors need to understand if the property is managing—and reducing—its waste and pollution.

All these factors can be measured in real time so that the situation can be analyzed for tactical and strategic measures to improve an asset's impact on the environment. Investors put much weight in these factors as leading indicators of a real estate investment's long-term sustainability and success.

What investors want: Social

A building is a physical space utilized in various ways by members of society—work, life, play. Even before the pandemic, the average person spent 90% of their time indoors, so the social aspects of a building and its management are important. Yet until now, social factors have often played second fiddle to environmental factors. Not anymore. After the experiences of 2020—pandemic-induced lockdowns and quarantines, and a renewed focus on inequality— investors are increasingly hungry for information about their real estate investments' social responsibility. Investors want to be assured that building managers comply with workplace health and safety guidelines. They want to know the air quality of a building. They want to be sure that there are no human rights violations or risks from the firm's suppliers and contractors. Investors need to be assured that the building and its management operate in a way that is fair and equitable to all members of society.

Increasingly, these factors are becoming measurable. More and more, investors want to know that their real estate investments are acting responsibly on social issues. Lack of performance in these areas is often seen by investors as potential litigation risks. For example, owners can be sued for inequitable hiring practices, or buildings can be picketed for discriminatory business practices such as refusing to rent to people of color or LGBTQ+ community members.

Social information is not just informative—it's now *actionable*. Much in the same way as energy usage and other environmental data, it has become critical to operators, owners, and investors alike.

What investors want: Governance

Any business requires effective governance, and real estate is no different. Investors need to be assured that the board structure and accountability of their investment is sound and follows the principles of corporate social responsibility and effective governance. They need to know that the firm follows proper accounting and disclosure practices, including an audit committee with independent auditors. Executive compensation must be transparent and fair.

For the governance factors of ESG, transparency is key. Investors will not risk their money in properties with opaque governance.

Global consulting and standards firm AccountAbility states that increasingly institutional investors will assert pressure on real estate companies to incorporate ESG into their corporate agendas, including finding ways to leverage sustainability as a method for enhancing business resilience and driving competitive advantages. The consultancy states that in the years to come, a greater emphasis will be on monetizing sustainability performance and investments, as well as adopting a more data-led and dynamic approach to ESG risk management and mitigation.[22]

AccountAbility raises an important point about the pressure investors put on real estate firms to change their behaviors. Investors are no longer passive stakeholders, content to sit on the sidelines and watch their assets grow. Increasingly they are resorting to activism to force businesses to change their behaviors—or risk the drying up of capital.

The rise of the ESG-conscious activist investor

Shareholder activism is the well-documented bane of corporate boards all around the globe. Often portrayed as corporate raiders who swoop in and strong-arm board members, so-called activist investors use equity stakes and shareholder voting as a way to pressure a company to change its behavior. When the average investor disagrees with a company's decision, she quietly divests of her shares and finds somewhere else to invest her capital. Not so the activist investor, who instead tenaciously attempts to influence the company to change its ways.

In its purest form, the activist's playbook is simple enough, and has its origins in the early 1600s, when an investor named Isaac Le Maire bought up shares in the first public company—the Dutch East India Company—and petitioned its board to disclose its accounts and pay shareholder dividends.[23] Today, activists will vigorously lobby or pressure corporate boards, C-suite executives, and other investors to get their way. Their tools are private communications with stakeholders or public censures in the form of lawsuits, proxy fights, and public relations campaigns.[24]

Famous activists of the modern era include such personalities as Elliott Management's Paul Singer, Greenlight Capital's David Einhorn, Pershing Square's Bill Ackman, Third Point's Daniel Loeb, and ValueAct Capital's founder Jeff Ubben. These hedge fund giants have led notable campaigns against companies such as AT&T,[25] Hyundai,[26] Walt Disney Company,[27] Microsoft,[28] Rolls-Royce,[29] and even fast-food restaurant chain Wendy's[30] in a bid to force companies to change their behaviors.

Activists can be prolific. According to figures from data provider Activist Insight, Elliott Management had targeted 64 companies with shareholder activism strategies between 2017 and 2020 alone. ValueAct targeted 13 in the same time period, Third Point 12, and Pershing three. Carl Icahn, often dubbed the 1980's original corporate raider and a pioneer of modern-day shareholder activism, targeted 18 companies for shareholder activism from 2017 to 2020.[31]

Icahn is the perennial example of how activist investors operate. In 1976 he wrote a letter to his investors, informing them that he would identify undervalued stocks and then profit by: "a) trying to convince management to liquidate or sell the company to a 'white knight' [a friendly buyer who would retain management]; b) waging a proxy contest [forcing issues to a vote in company annual meetings]; c) making a tender offer and/or; d) selling back our position to the company."[32]

In recent years Icahn has unleashed his strategy on companies such as Motorola, Yahoo! Inc, Netflix, Dell, Apple, and eBay. Between 2007 and 2010, Icahn used a proxy contest to win representation on Motorola's board, issued public statements and letters to shareholders, and threatened litigation of a company he felt was "passively failing" to reach its potential. In the end he orchestrated the spin off and sale of parts of the company to Google for a 63% premium over closing price. From 2013 to 2016, Icahn waged war with Apple, issuing public statements (including tweets) about the need for the cash-rich tech giant to distribute cash to shareholders. In April 2013, Apple bowed to Wall Street pressure to return $100 billion to shareholders by the end of 2015. While the amount was double what it had previously pledged, Icahn believed it was still too little. Icahn began accumulating shares and issuing statements that Apple should release $150 billion. Ultimately, Apple released $130 billion by the end of 2015.[33]

Once seen as a pariah, by 2014 Icahn and his ilk were championed by a host of surprising stakeholders as an important part of the capital markets. Then-SEC Chair Mary Jo White commented early that year that shareholder activism had lost its "distinctly negative connotation," and *The Economist* observed that activists "help to improve corporate performance by stirring up much-needed debate about strategy and leadership, just as in democracies the government of a country is improved by the existence of an effective opposition."[34]

Proponents of sustainable investing have taken a page out of the shareholder activist's playbook to push companies to do better on ESG factors.

On January 6, 2018, New York-based activist hedge fund Jana Partners co-wrote a letter with the California State Teachers' Retirement System (CalSTRS) to Apple, imploring the company to "offer parents more choices and tools to help them ensure that young consumers are using your products in an optimal manner." Citing academic research, the hedge fund and teachers' pension claimed that child overuse of iPhones was linked to inattention in the classroom, difficulty empathizing, depression, sleep deprivation, and a higher risk of suicide.[35] Between them, Jana and CalSTRS controlled around $2 billion in Apple shares, and the two investors argued that unless the tech firm addressed their concerns, its reputation and stock could be hurt. While CalSTRS had a reputation for ESG investing, Jana was known as a strong activist which would lobby hard on financial matters, and this was the first time it had publicly pressed a company on an issue of social responsibility.[36]

In an article for the Harvard Business Review, Oxford University Saïd Business School professor Robert Eccles asked (and answered) his own question about Jana's move: "How is it that sharp-toothed activists are becoming advocates of long-term sustainable investing? A main explanation is that, as always, they are following the money."[37] Eccles noted the Apple letter as a sign that the worlds of activism and impact investing were converging "much more swiftly than most people realize."

Other hard-nosed practitioners of corporate raiding have also turned their sights on companies that refuse to follow sustainability principles. Ubben stepped down as CEO of ValueAct in June 2020 to launch Inclusive Capital Partners as an ESG-focused activist fund.[38] By the end of the third quarter of that year, his new fund topped the leaderboard of hedge fund activists by a wide margin.[39] Ubben's rationale for launching a sustainable hedge fund provides a poignant example of the change in attitude among many bastions of capitalism.

Speaking about his decision at the Bloomberg Green Festival in September 2020, Ubben (59 at the time) said: "I'm on a crusade. I'm late in life. I've got five years to fix the harm I've done... We thought we would go on boards and make companies more financially healthy, and we would get an idiosyncratic return for that. That is what we did, and to a certain extent we caused the harm. We ourselves, I think, built unsustainable companies by maximizing profit."

At the beginning of 2021, a group of investors representing more than $54 trillion in capital voiced their concerns that corporations were not doing enough to clear their short- and medium-term carbon reduction targets. The 545 global investors from 33 markets called out 167 firms they said drive 80% of global industrial emissions. The investors were part of a carbon emissions benchmarking group called Climate Action 100+. "We will be using it not only to inform our engagement, but also our proxy voting," Anne Simpson, managing investment director of board governance and sustainability at CalPERS said at a briefing on the announcement on March 22. "For us, ultimately, we have to be able to hold boards accountable for delivering the strategy, that CapEx [capital expenditure], the compensation plans, the approach to political lobbying, and the regular reporting, so that we've got confidence that they're on track."[40]

Dutch pension fund PGGM has been a strong climate activist for many years. Between January 2006 and August 2008, PGGM supported 48 shareholder motions that asked 28 U.S. and two Japanese companies for more climate-friendly policy.[41] By 2015 it voted in 30 proxy contests, dissenting against the board 43% of the time.[42] In 2019 the pension fund teamed up with German reinsurer Munich Re to analyze climate risk on the 4,000 real estate holdings within its portfolio. The data gleaned is used by PGGM to identify risks and pressure asset owners to enact mitigation.[43]

The number of ESG-focused activist funds is growing. These firms specifically campaign on sustainability principles by using the shareholder activist's tools of the trade. One of the first activist ESG funds was Zevin Asset Management—a Boston-based sustainable and responsible investment manager founded in 1997 by former Vietnam War activist Robert Zevin. In 2020, the firm had 558 clients and managed around $519 million.[44] Zevin has a long history of pushing companies to better adhere to sustainability principles. In 2019, Zevin voted on 3,915 corporate annual meeting proposals, supporting shareholder-led proposals 94% of the time and supporting management compensation proposals only 38% of the time. In its annual Impact Report, the manager said that in most cases, votes were against company directors when the board lacked racial or gender diversity, or if CEO pay packages were exorbitant or not sufficiently tied to performance metrics.[45] In recent years, Zevin's activism has included:

- Campaigning for AT&T to take measure to reduce emissions from its large auto fleet
- Spurring PepsiCo and CVS Health to commit to science-based greenhouse gas targets
- Helping convince UPS to set a quantitative target for sourcing renewable electricity and more sustainable fuels
- Convincing travel site Priceline's owner to publish its first-ever sustainability report.[46]

While the market and economic effects of the Covid-19 pandemic effectively put a pause on shareholder activism in 2020, the first quarter of 2021 saw a return to business as normal, with a marked increase in proxy activity and shareholder proposals. Significantly, there was also a marked increase in ESG-specific shareholder activism. Commentators and experts in the field forecast ESG to move into the center stage of shareholder activism in the future.

In a note to clients in early 2021, law firm White and Case warned corporations that ESG issues were set to increasingly influence the activist agenda. The law firm observed that the events of 2020—the global pandemic and rise of the Black Lives Matter movement—brought ESG issues into sharp focus, including rising concerns over climate change, social inequality, and diversity issues.

"Companies that are lagging behind the pack in ESG ratings risk lowering their valuations, and as such have become prime targets for activists," the lawyers wrote. "As a result, ESG issues will increasingly drive activists' investment theses and campaign rhetoric—particularly when it comes to issues of sustainability and board diversity."[47]

Yet it is the normalization of ESG activism that may be the greatest sign of the times. In February 2021, law firm Skadden, Arps, Slate, Meagher & Flom told clients that activists were raising permanent capital in a bid to give them greater leverage, and that ESG activist approaches were increasingly more acceptable to a wider range of institutional investors. "Even high-performing companies may face pressure on ESG issues," the law firm warned.[48]

The warning came as a new player rose in ESG activism.

Such as Climate Action 100+, Net Zero Asset Managers is a global group of institutional investors formed to pressure companies to reduce their carbon emissions. Specifically, its members want corporations to support "the goal of net zero greenhouse gas emissions by 2050 or sooner, in line with global efforts to limit warming to 1.5 degrees Celsius."[49] Money managed by members of the activist group tripled in early 2021 and at the time encompassed over a third of the total assets under management worldwide.[50] As the money flowed in, giving the group more teeth, Net Zero called on corporations to provide more transparency on their carbon footprints and emission reduction plans, vowing to take action if they did not.[51]

ESG shareholder activism has now become mainstream—no longer the domain of a few corporate raiders. Even the most traditional real estate firms use activism to promote their ESG policies.

Heitman's Laura Craft says her firm can—and does—use shareholder activism as part of its toolkit to ensure companies live up to its ESG standards.

"We engage with listed companies that we invest in and we make sure we use our shareholder's vote," Craft says. "We maintain relationships with the management of the REITs we invest in and we engage regularly on ESG issues to make sure ESG is integrated within their firm."

With the rise in prominence of ESG as a target for activist investors, and shareholder activism no longer the tool of corporate raiders, real estate companies need to understand the severe risk these developments pose.

Yet perhaps the greatest existential risk to real estate companies— besides climate change itself—may be coming not from shareholders, but instead from the increasing pressure of regulatory frameworks and laws.

The new regulatory landscape

Commercial real estate accounts for 18% of all carbon emissions[52] and is already one of the most regulated industries. Real estate in its entirety (including single family residential) accounts for 40% of all carbon emissions,[53] so it is little wonder that governments—especially in countries that have signed the Paris Agreement on climate change—are increasingly choosing to regulate real estate companies.

Many legal and environmental experts believe laws aimed at protecting the environment and encouraging sustainable practices are set to see significant growth in the next few years.[54] At the time of writing this book, in the early stages of the Biden presidency in the United States, legal commentators were forecasting the Administration would dramatically expand regulations protecting the environment, as well as escalate the use of litigation to punish bad actors.[55]

Regulation affecting the built environment comes in two main categories—the regulation of how buildings are constructed and maintained, and the regulation of the companies that own real estate. Below are a few key examples of each type of regulation, followed by a discussion of how companies can mitigate regulatory risk.

Rules for construction and maintenance of buildings

Building codes touch on all aspects of the construction and maintenance of properties, from the materials that can—and cannot—be used in construction, to mandating certain types of toilets be installed to improve water usage efficiency. However, with carbon emissions being a primary concern of governments, much of the focus of sustainable regulations is on energy usage.

In the United States, a key regulatory driver of how buildings are constructed and maintained is the U.S. Department of Energy. For over 20 years its Office Energy Efficiency & Renewable Energy has developed model building energy codes, compliance, and enforcement practices to encourage states and local authorities to modernize construction regulations. The scheme is part of the government's long-running goal of national energy savings and reduction of carbon emissions.

According to the Department of Energy, as of March 2021 eight states had adopted the most recent building energy code standards for commercial building construction (released in 2016) and 15 states had adopted the previous codes (released in 2013). Only four states—Arizona, Hawaii, Maine, and Oklahoma—were yet to adopt modern building energy codes (regulations written later than 2007).[56]

Many states and large American cities are taking the lead on implementing building codes that bake in principles of sustainability and ESG.

California was the first state to enact a mandatory Green building standards code. In 2007, it developed Green building standards as part of statewide measures to reduce greenhouse gasses to 1990 levels by 2020. The state's Building Standards Commission proposes "CALGreen" standards for nonresidential new buildings, additions, and alterations.[57] The codes encourage—with compliance and enforcement measures—sustainable construction practices in the planning and design stages, energy efficiency, water conservation, material and resource efficiency, and the environmental quality of the built environment.

On the East Coast, New York City Local Law 87 requires buildings in the city over 50,000 gross square feet to have periodic energy audits and improve the efficiency of their equipment and systems—a measure known as retro-commissioning. The city ordinance is part of New York's "Greener, Greater Buildings Plan" (GGBP).[58]

On the other side of the Atlantic, in 2010 the European Union passed the Energy Performance of Buildings Directive, which requires Member States to "set minimum requirements for the energy performance of buildings and building elements."[59]

In early 2021, as the continent began healing from the global Coronavirus pandemic, the EU sought to link economic recovery with improvements in Europe's sustainability. Top of mind in Brussels was a large expansion of building renovations to improve energy efficiency across the region.

While stopping short of making the minimum energy performance standards legally binding on Member States, the move did tie the EU's €750 billion COVID-19 economic recovery fund to countries making a concerted effort to renovate buildings to improve energy efficiency.[60] The intended trickle-down effect is that companies seeking to renovate buildings will be encouraged to use sustainable methods and materials.

Regulating real estate companies

Real estate companies—especially those listed on a stock exchange—are required to follow the same governance standards as all businesses. As we saw in Chapter 1, the SEC requires companies to disclose sustainability information. While it does not prescribe a specific format for how to disclose, there are a number of standard frameworks followed, including the Sustainability Accounting Standards Board and the Task Force on Climate-related Financial Disclosures.

Failure to disclose material sustainability information does not only present an impediment to raising capital. It also comes with the risk of enforcement action in the form of punitive fines. While these rules may have been less enforced in the past, the tide seems to be turning. In March, the SEC announced the formation of a Climate and ESG Task Force operating within its Division of Enforcement. The task force's remit is to proactively identify "ESG-related misconduct" and go after bad actors. It will also use "sophisticated data analysis" to identify potential violations in ESG disclosure—material gaps or misstatements in the disclosure of climate risks under the SEC's rules.[61]

On March 10, 2021, the European Union's Sustainable Finance Disclosure Regulation (SFDR) became effective. The directive imposes sustainability-related disclosure requirements on banks, insurance companies, investment firms, and pension funds. These institutional investors must now be transparent about: how much sustainability risk assessment is integrated into their decision-making and due diligence, how adverse sustainability impacts their investments, and the overall sustainability of their financial products.

European regulation may seem an ocean away from U.S. markets, but experts say it will nonetheless add to the growing call for American corporations to disclose ESG data more systematically on their operations. U.S. asset managers that sell funds in Europe must comply with SFDR, which means they are required to disclose ESG information about their underlying holdings—the companies and real estate assets contained in their funds.[62]

Rhys Davies, a lawyer at global law firm DLA Piper and a specialist in sustainability law, says SFDR is a useful example of how many regulatory frameworks are approaching sustainability.

"It is heavy with taxonomies that provide companies with metrics to tell governments and investors how Green they are. Investment firms are required to provide a 'Principal Adverse Impacts' statement to flag their sustainability challenges. While this might be unpopular with the business community, watchdogs and investors will probably find these regulations helpful in weeding out risky investments. These types of regulatory frameworks are not overly concerned with companies telling them how good they are—they view upside as the domain of the capital markets. Instead, they require companies to disclose their sustainability problems," says Davies.

The U.S. view of sustainability disclosure regulation is somewhat different, says Davies. As already mentioned, the SEC does not currently provide a specific taxonomy or framework for sustainability disclosure. Instead, it permits companies to choose how they present information related to their ESG policies and risks.

"This approach to regulation seems to be saying that there does not need to be a prescribed framework. Instead, companies can rely on the market's preexisting understanding of what is material to divulge, based on what the market thinks is important for the investor to know. Such a view enlarges the concept of what should be in the information pool for investors to make a decision. However, it does not provide a framework for evaluating what is good behavior," says Davies. "Europe's approach is to demand specific disclosure in a specific way. The SEC leaves it up to the companies to decide, and therefore relies more on the market to self-regulate. Probably the optimum approach is somewhere between the two."

The SEC has recently begun to admit it may need to do more to protect investors. On March 15, 2021, acting chair Allison Herren Lee revealed the SEC was examining how it could implement more uniformity in sustainability reporting. However, Herren Lee also emphasized that it was the place of the shareholder to "exercise oversight of the companies they own and the funds in which they invest through certain fundamental rights."[63]

Davies believes European-style safeguards such as the Principal Adverse Impact approach are useful because they reveal what is not working in a business—what are the risks. The American approach is more about understanding and driving the right culture in a business—what are the rewards. However, Davies thinks the market also needs common metrics that encourage companies to be better actors.

One organization attempting to do just that is the World Economic Forum, which in June 2020 named its 50th annual meeting the "Great Reset." At this meeting, the WEF embraced a concept recently popularized by influential experts such as Mark Carney, the former Bank of England Governor and United Nations special envoy for climate action and finance: Stakeholder Capitalism.

As we covered in Chapter 1, the concept is a direct rebuke of Friedman's insistence that companies exist purely to maximize shareholder value. Instead, stakeholder capitalism asks companies to also take into consideration the needs of customers, employees, local communities, and suppliers.

In 2020, the WEF set about building a framework of common metrics and consistent reporting to show a company's "Sustainable Value Creation."[64]

Davies believes the WEF's approach is typical of the middle ground of compliance and regulatory initiatives.

"These frameworks—often led by business groups rather than regulators—attempt to provide common metrics for reporting both the good and the bad," he says.

Whatever the regulatory approach—emphasizing the positives and negatives, or taking the middle ground—Davies believes that the rigor of reporting comes not from the narrative a company is trying to tell, but instead from the data it uses to evidence that story.

"It is the data that provides the transparency that both the regulators and the markets need to comprehend the true nature of a company's sustainability risks—and its opportunities," says Davies. "But that's easier said than done and raises some serious concerns about how companies can utilize a set of metrics that are auditable, capable of assurance across the entirety of the ESG spectrum, and will satisfy both the regulators and the market."

Risk is front and center

Regulatory and legal risk are far more of a concern for real estate businesses than they ever were. And for very good reason. After the effects of the global Coronavirus pandemic, health and safety has risen to ever greater importance for building users. As the Black Lives Matter and #MeToo movements drew attention to society's endemic inequality, the general public also turned its attention to the importance of the S in ESG. Society is rightly placing more of an emphasis on health, safety, and equality. They are using not just their power as consumers, but also the power of the legal system itself to enforce these views.

Against this backdrop, companies are increasingly called on to include reputational—and even moral and ethical—issues in their day-to-day tactical decisions and long-term business strategy. Corporate survival demands businesses respond to the wave of societal, cultural, and economic events of the past decade. Companies are increasingly being asked to take what they see as an ethical stand to protect themselves from litigation and regulatory strife, and to deflect potential knocks to their reputation.[65] In this environment, legal and regulatory considerations are becoming even more central to the company's strategy and reputation.

Davies says that as regulators increase their emphasis on enforcement actions, many companies might get caught on the back foot if they are not proactive about improving their ESG performance.

"Many companies still hold the view that regulation is an imposition on business. As a result, they decide to comply no more and no less than they have to. A focus by regulators on fines and punishment reinforces that view," says Davies.

Worse still, Davies believes a greater emphasis on enforcement will not affect the change required in corporate sensibilities to make companies more attuned to ESG principles.

"The more regulatory intervention there is in this space, the more it might actually exacerbate the problems we have; the traditional risk mindset tells you that if you comply with the law, you are therefore meeting societal expectations. And that's not the case. It has probably never been the case," Davies says.

Many experts support this view, fearing that by emphasizing sustainability reporting, the market is confusing the output of reports with the actual impact that a company might make. In fact, in the last 20 years, while sustainability reporting and investing has increased dramatically, so too have carbon emissions and environmental damage.[66]

One of the solutions, says Davies, is for businesses to proactively show that they are responding to ESG risks in a systemic way.

"The whack-a-mole method of responding to regulatory intervention does not lead to companies formulating a systemic strategy for effecting positive, lasting change," says Davies. "You are not a sustainable company just because you have dodged a fine or complied with the latest regulation. Such thinking lulls businesses into a false sense of security."

For real estate owners and operators, it is clear that there are a vast range of risks that need to be dealt with in both tactical and strategic ways. These include physical climate risks such as floods, hurricanes, and wildfires. They are financial, such as credit exposure and higher insurance premiums. They are reputational, such as ignoring social norms. And they are regulatory and legal from noncompliance of laws and the expectations of society.

Real estate owners, operators, and investors will no longer tolerate these risks. They are too expensive. So, it is normal for real estate owners to try to mitigate them as best they can. Whatever the debate is on the reward side—that better ESG performance leads to cost savings, efficiencies, and improved access to capital—the punitive side of poor ESG performance is arguably as existential. Yet simply trying to avoid risk is no lasting solution. Risk mitigation requires a proactive approach.

Tenants lead the charge

There is another risk to real estate companies that has been gaining ground for the better part of the last three decades: Tenant expectations. Along with lack of access to capital, the risk of being unable to attract tenants because of deficiencies in a building's ESG compliance represents an exceptional threat to many real estate businesses.

I believe we are quickly coming to a time when good tenants simply will not rent a building if it is not Green enough. At the same time investors and regulators have become agents of change in the adoption of ESG principles in the real estate market, the users of buildings have also increasingly exerted their influence. Today, tenants—following their own ESG agendas and objectives—are taking a more selective approach and demanding more from the spaces they occupy, either out of ethical considerations or because their organization's compliance obligations require it.

As a broker in San Diego, I represented a medical device maker in 2009 that was looking to rent a property for offices and a manufacturing plant. They had a special request. The CEO wondered if I could find him a property with rooftop solar panels. The cost savings of solar power was not the only criteria on his mind. By attempting to become more Green, the CEO felt that he could enhance his brand and attract and retain a better quality of staff. I was impressed with his thinking, but quietly worried that prospective landlords might balk at the prospect of the extra infrastructure outlay.

Yet many of the landlords I approached welcomed the idea and were keen to accommodate such a forward-thinking tenant. Many believed it was an astute investment for their building. The deal we eventually made structured the request into the lease, with the landlord initially paying for the solar panels and the cost amortized into the tenant's lease payments. This was the first time that I remember having a tenant-initiated discussion about Green building concepts such as renewable energy. Yet it is now just one of many examples I have seen over the years of a tenant's ESG criteria impacting the terms of a lease.

Often tenants want building searches to be filtered by ENERGY STAR ratings or LEED certification, yet often this is only the baseline for their demands.

Eventually, I began running CBRE's sustainability practice group and organized a group of brokers interested in sustainable leasing practices. We would have monthly calls to discuss best practices and how to help clients achieve their sustainability goals. This was a forward-thinking, innovative group of real estate professionals. However, increasingly we would find Old School brokers showing up on these calls, wishing to discuss the curious new demands of their corporate tenants. These traditional tenant representatives had little interest in sustainable business, but their large corporate clients were increasingly making demands that they could not accommodate—LEED certified retrofits, Green Lease clauses, and energy efficiency commitments. These were just good old-fashioned brokers doing middle-market 60,000-100,000 ft. industrial and office space leases, but their tenants' needs were changing dramatically. Today, these types of brokers could not work with high-profile companies such as Google, Apple, Facebook, VMware, Bank of America, or any of the top Fortune 500 companies without understanding Green and sustainability requirements in leases.

Tenant demands for Green leases have an interesting origin. In 1992, President George H.W. Bush signed the Energy Policy Act, which aimed to reduce American dependence on energy imports, increase the country's renewable energy production, and improve the energy efficiency of buildings.[67] As the world's largest owner, operator, and lessee of real estate,[68] President Bush wanted the Federal government to take the lead in improving energy efficiency. To this end, the new Act required Federal agencies to reduce their energy use by 35% by 2010.

To achieve this, the Act compelled the Federal government to not only evaluate the energy efficiency of the buildings it owned, but also to include energy efficiency considerations into current and future leases.[69] A bill previously signed by Bush—the Clean Air Act 1990—paved the way for the Energy Star rating system, and the new energy bill encouraged the use of such metrics. Executive Orders from subsequent presidents—particularly Bill Clinton (EO-13123[70]), George W. Bush (EO-13423[71]) and Barack Obama (EO-13693[72])—added to Federal government requirements to consider sustainability when leasing property (including the eventual requirement that leased buildings attain LEED certification). By 2010, the U.S. General Services Administration (which handles non-military property leasing for the Federal government) raised the certification requirement to LEED Gold.[73]

Since 1992, the two largest tenants in America—the Department of Defense and the GSA—have both required that their landlords meet high levels of energy efficiency and sustainability.

While many may only think of sustainability as a relatively recent demand of tenants, it has been around for a very long time. In the United States, the Federal government has led the way for almost 30 years in tenant demands for sustainability. What is beginning to change now is not necessarily the ethical beliefs behind those demands, but instead the requirement that landlords provide quantifiable proof of their sustainability beyond mere Green certification.

The Federal government, Fortune 500 companies, smart startups, and now residential lessors are all desiring Green and sustainable spaces.[74] So, if you are a landlord, what do you do with this information? The answer requires little deliberation: You meet the customer's needs.

Society starts shaping the real estate agenda

Over the past few years public discourse and beliefs on the need for sustainability and ESG have pushed companies to do more to protect the environment. As communities fall prey to increasingly harsh climate and weather conditions, the calls have increased. In California, home to America's most dangerous wildfire season, power company Pacific Gas & Electric—a sizable real estate owner in its own right— filed for bankruptcy in January 2019, for fear it would be unable to pay an expected $30bn in damages to wildfire victims.[75] At the time, the case was the largest bankruptcy ever in California and the sixth largest in the country. Many of the 70,000 claimants lost their homes entirely in fires caused by the state's most devastating wildfire in 2018—blamed on PG&E equipment failures. Australia too has recently suffered severe loss from bushfires. Estimates for insured losses in 2019 and 2020 are around $1.441 billion. About 24 million hectares of that country's land was burned between September 2019 and March 2020.[76]

Water usage has also become a hot button issue for society—especially in areas where water is in short supply. In April 2021, the City of Las Vegas began pushing a ban on ornamental grass. At the time, the Southern Nevada Water Authority estimated that ornamental grass required around four times as much water as drought-tolerant landscaping such as cacti and succulents. By ridding city and private properties of such turf, the utility believed Las Vegans could reduce annual water consumption by 15% and save 14 gallons per person a day.[77]

Public discourse took on a world-altering dimension in 2020 when two seismic events shook the globe: The worldwide Coronavirus pandemic and a renewed focus on racial inequality as a result of efforts from the Black Lives Matter movement.

As early as March of that year, prior to nationwide lockdowns in many Western countries, experts were warning that the state of many buildings' infrastructure and systems posed a health threat to residents and workers. In a March 4 *New York Times* opinion piece, Dr. Joseph Allen, director of Harvard University's Healthy Buildings program, warned that improper ventilation, ineffective filtration, and high levels of humidity in buildings helps spread pathogens such as the coronavirus. He recommended real estate operators bring in more outdoor air with heating and ventilation systems instead of recirculating air, utilize air purification technology, and decrease humidity levels.[78]

Since then, asset owners have gone to great lengths to show tenants that they have heeded such warnings and put tenant health and safety first. Owners of aging condominiums are upgrading their HVAC systems to relieve tenant fears.[79] New office constructions nearing completion during the pandemic began specifically implementing—and marketing—anti-COVID features, such as doors that hold open (so that they do not need to be touched so often) and bathrooms with a single path of travel.[80] In March 2021, the World Health Organization released a roadmap to better ventilation, providing targets and measures that buildings can implement.[81]

In February 2021, trade publication *Buildings Magazine* summed up nicely the imperative for building owners at the time: "Workers will soon be coming back to the office. These people will be educated on the dangers of airborne transmission of COVID-19 and understandably concerned about indoor air quality (IAQ). They will look to you—the building owners and facilities managers—for all kinds of reassurances that new systems are now in place to improve IAQ and prevent viral spread. You need to be able to talk the talk. More importantly, you need to know whether these newly installed prevention measures are working."[82]

While the idea of utilizing technology and data to improve energy efficiency in buildings had been around for a while, the pandemic broadened the conversation to include issues of health and safety. The message was clear, as articulated in technology trade magazine *IoT World Today*: "Smart building features can ease sales cycles and boost customer satisfaction compared with conventional buildings."[83]

So too has racial inequality become an important issue for the real estate industry as society places greater importance on equality. The Black Lives Matter movement (BLM) began out of indignation over the acquittal of George Zimmerman in the 2012 shooting and death of Trayvon Martin, a Black teenager, in Florida. In response to the acquittal, three Black female organizers tweeted the hashtag #blacklivesmatter. After the murders of two more Black men in 2014—Michael Brown and Eric Garner—the movement began growing nationally.[84] In 2020, two more murders—Breonna Taylor and George Floyd—sparked a swell of support for the movement and international protests against police killings of Black people specifically, and institutionalized racial inequality generally. The movement is thought to be the largest in American history, with data suggesting that in May and June 2020, 15 million to 26 million people participated in demonstrations related to the movement.[85]

A protest movement initially focused on police shootings quickly evolved into an international conversation about racial inequality in all its forms. At the height of the Coronavirus pandemic, statistics showed that Black people were dying disproportionately of the virus.[86] As BLM co-founder Patrisse Cullors puts it: "When we say Black Lives Matter, we're talking about more than police brutality. We're talking about incarceration, health care, *housing*, education, and economics—all the different components of a broader system that has created the reality we see today…"[87]

Part of this conversation is about racial equality in real estate. Legal and industry experts alike believe that systemic racism exists explicitly and implicitly in U.S. housing policies and commercial practices. They can be found in zoning and housing laws,[88] in preferences given to white renters over renters of color,[89] and in the hiring practices of some real estate companies (Black Americans represent less than 6% of real estate professionals).[90] In early 2021, Black home ownership rates were around 44%, while the white ownership rate was closer to 74%.[91]

The events of 2020 underscored the atrocity of climate and racial inequality in our economic decision making. So, it is no surprise that these issues would disproportionately impact the real estate business, since property is the largest asset class on the planet. Property is also one of the most socially and environmentally impactful features of society—as a species, we spend the vast majority of our time living, working, and playing indoors.

In a world where landlords are competing to lure tenants to their buildings, they need to enrich that experience and address the concerns and reservations people have about health, well-being, and equality.

But real estate owners, operators, and investors are also members of a broader society that must ask itself some hard questions. It is incumbent on all of us to be better. And we can only improve when we can identify the problem, measure it, and commit to making things better.

Less cautionary tale, more success story

Investor activism, regulatory risk, tenant demands, and an evolutionary shift in the public discourse may sound frightening. But this is not just a story about the skyrocketing costs of building improvements and the dire risks of unequal business practices. There are opportunities to be had for astute operators who understand the power of ESG metrics to monitor their businesses and guide their strategies.

Operators who can navigate the winds of change will always do well after a dramatic shift in society. We have already seen this happen to a certain degree during the Coronavirus crisis. During the pandemic, online retail received a significant boost, which may have decreased the value of physical shopfronts but increased the value of logistics operations and warehouses. It is possible the future of retail may have more in common with industrial shipping than it will experiential shopping.

However, with careful attention to ESG factors such as energy efficiency, air quality, cleanliness and hygiene, and spatial awareness, retail stores offering experiential shopping could do very well compared to the competition. The profound shifts in the way that we utilize space will continue to be a problem for those who cannot keep up, and an opportunity for those who can innovate.

The economic crisis caused by the pandemic has also opened opportunities to improve the economy's sustainability. When workers fled their offices for safety at home—whether voluntarily or mandated by lockdowns—landlords around the world took the chance to upgrade their vacant buildings. They retrofitted them with more energy-efficient lighting. They installed solar panels. They prepared for the inevitable return to work with improved air circulator technology.

Governments designed economic stimulus packages to encourage such improvements. In the U.S., the Biden Administration tied its COVID stimulus for businesses with financial support from green grants, green loans, and green bonds. The green money was to be used to encourage Green innovations and investments that would help companies financially recover from the pandemic while also baking sustainability and racial equality into their businesses.[92] Similarly, in early 2021 the European Union unveiled an €800 billion recovery plan that included up to €250 billions of green bonds to finance environmentally beneficial projects.[93] Essentially, both the EU and the U.S. were saying to the business community: "You can have this money, but you need to be more efficient in your carbon emissions. Use this money to recover from the pandemic but do it in a way that is more sustainable."

In a world wracked by a global pandemic, real estate owners are fighting adversity, managing risk, and being disrupted by changes in how society uses interior space. To be competitive in such a highly dynamic environment requires embracing technology; Low energy lighting, photovoltaic energy, water leak sensors, air purification technology—there is a raft of proven technology to help operators decarbonize their buildings and improve costs. There are also business systems and ESG data monitors that can help asset owners monitor performance, report regulatory compliance, and meet investor expectations.

It is natural for companies to try and save money during a crisis, and in the early days of the 2020 pandemic, many real estate owners did just that, effectively going into the foxhole until it was clear to come back out again. However, as the pandemic wore on, many came to view the moment as an opportunity. Vacant buildings could be retrofitted and improved without disturbing tenants. Projects that were scheduled to take years could be completed in mere months. Smart real estate operators made the crisis work for them.

Such behavior is not new. It is exactly what many asset owners did during the global financial crisis of 2008. While many industry commentators heralded the global recession as the end of Green building, in fact it became a motivator for building improvements. The years directly after the global financial crisis not only saw steady growth in the U.S. Green building market, but also a boom in LEED certification.[94] It is foreseeable that the next few late-and-post-pandemic years will see a similar burst of activity in the real estate sector. The difference this time will be that some companies will have the metrics and the insight to make incisive strategic decisions that will help their properties outperform.

And crucially, some companies will not.

Chapter 3:

You Cannot Manage What You Do Not Measure

Society, industry—and very soon the planet—has reached the point of no return. Green certification will no longer be what drives change in sustainability. The future requires objective, transparent measures of real estate value, an equation in which ESG metrics are now variables. This transformation builds on the definitions, standards, and evangelism Green certification organizations achieved but is no longer predicated on decals. It's based on data.

The Building Research Establishment Environmental Assessment Methodology (BREEAM) and Leadership in Energy and Environmental Design (LEED) certification frameworks that grew up in the 1990s based on the tenets of the Green building movement provided us with the foundations to talk about "Green". These frameworks raised awareness about the importance of evaluating the greenness of an asset. But certifications—with their binary view of an asset being "certified" or "not certified"—have taken us as far as they are able. A time is coming—in fact it is arguably already here—when Green certification ceases to be able to drive positive change, or to accurately reflect the sustainability of a real estate asset. What is needed now is a new, more dynamic model of measurement.

The limits of certification

While the British-based Green certification BREEAM launched before the American version, LEED—and some would argue is a better certification framework than its cousin—there is a simple reason why LEED is the most popular Green building certification on the planet: it has the superior marketing strategy.

Americans are very good at exporting brands, whether it be McDonalds, Coca-Cola, or Ford. LEED is yet another great example of American prowess at exporting a successful product. With great marketing and a compelling story, LEED has been able to spread the word about the importance of evaluating whether a building is Green or not—at least Green or not at *a particular moment in time* (but we'll dig into that later).

LEED and other certification providers are skilled storytellers with long experience communicating the importance of judging a building on the merits of how closely it conforms to Green building and sustainability practices. And the world is better for this message. Without certification providers trumpeting the importance of sustainability, it is hard to imagine asset owners, let alone the construction industry, embracing the concept as much as they have so far.

However, it's worth thinking about the business model behind providing certifications, and how it may not be as altogether altruistic as it might first appear. In fact, you don't have to dig too deeply before it becomes apparent that the idea of Green that certification companies expound reflects a specific point of view.

Green building certifications providers are selling a marketing tool. The marketing tool they sell is a plaque in the building's lobby and a certificate in the boardroom which reads "Certified Green." Certification is a for-profit business. Building owners must pay for their certification, and it is in the certification company's best interests to endorse as many buildings as they possibly can.

Now, that is not to say that certification companies do not have high standards. Many do. Without high standards, their products would be devalued. Certification companies have spent decades establishing their authority and developing a complex set of criteria for measurement and evaluation of a building's greenness. But it is undeniable that if building owners did not pay for their accreditation, certification companies would not have a business.

In simplistic terms, the price for certification—the money that asset owners pay to become certified Green—derives from a number of sub-services that are offered during the lifecycle of a certification project. First comes the initial application fee. Next comes an extensive evaluation across several categories, funded by the applicant. Upon successful completion of the assessment, a report is prepared. If the report is favorable (i.e. recommending approval) there will be a fee for certification. If the report is unfavorable (for instance, a building doesn't qualify at all, or does not meet the requirements for the desired level of certification, such as Gold or Platinum) there may be a (sometimes lengthy and costly) appeals process. Without subjecting themselves to the evaluation process—and paying a fee for the privilege—asset owners cannot obtain certification.

To say that certification companies have a vested interest is not to say there is no value in the service they have historically offered. Without them, the belief in the value of building sustainably would likely not be as prevalent as it is today, and the construction industry would not have moved as far towards sustainability as it has. Certification companies effectively promulgated the idea that there is economic and societal value in constructing buildings with a view toward protecting the environment, scarce resources, and the societies that the buildings serve as places to live, work, and play.

Green building certification companies also provide a benchmark for the construction or retrofitting of a property on completion of work. Developers can use these benchmarks to ensure their projects conform to sustainability practices. A Green certification is the articulation of a single thought: that at a certain point in time, a specific building was deemed to conform to a certain set of criteria—a certain notion of Green. And that notion is subjective.

Green certifications were born to fill a gap in the market. They rose up out of a vacuum of information on what it is to be Green, and how property developers could improve practices to build more sustainably. The movement began with the notion that there were non-Green assets and there were Green assets. If an asset was Green, it would be certified. And if an asset wasn't certified, it was not a Green asset.

In the beginning of Green certification, the criteria were similarly straightforward: Don't pollute, be energy efficient, try to consider the environment, and we'll give you a stamp of approval. Certification companies were so good at their marketing that this binary idea was what the market believed for quite some time.

But the reality is that the world is not binary. Nothing is Green or not Green. Everything exists on a spectrum. At a certain point in time, certification companies began to acknowledge this basic truth by formulating a sliding scale of certification ratings—for instance Certified, Silver, Gold, and Platinum. Yet the binary nature of certification persisted, and the narrative continued that if a building was not certified, then it must not be Green.

The green certification market is a business

It is worth taking a moment to review the most popular certification and assessment programs around the world. Notice how much they differ in terms of price, categories covered, and the methods for evaluations. It is striking how different the methodologies and price can be for what is effectively the same product—a certification of "Green".

BOMA 360 and BOMA Best

The Building Owners and Managers Association (BOMA) provides a building designation program called BOMA 360 for occupied commercial and industrial buildings. BOMA markets their certification product as recognizing "excellence in building operations and management" based on "industry best practices."

"Earning the prestigious BOMA 360 label demonstrates that a building is outperforming the competition across all areas of operations and management," says its marketing material.[1]

In 2021, fees ranged from $900 for BOMA members to $1,140 for non-members for buildings under 100,000 square feet, to $1,800 for members to $2,280 for non-members for buildings above 600,000 square feet.[2]

For office buildings, BOMA 360[3] grades properties in six categories, providing a points system for each category:

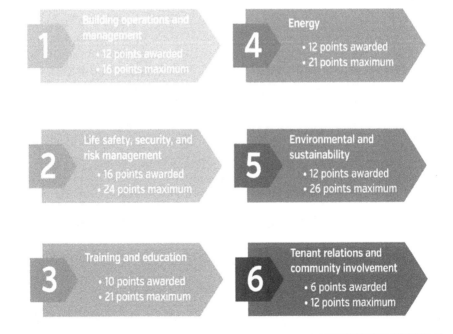

BOMA Canada has its own environmental assessment and certification program for existing buildings. The Canadian branch of BOMA calls its certification BOMA Best. The Canadian system has several different assessment modules, depending on the type of building—shopping centers, office buildings, residential complexes, etc.—and five levels of certification: Certified, Bronze, Silver, Gold, and Platinum. Grades are allocated depending on the score the building achieves on a questionnaire. For instance, Bronze is awarded to buildings that achieve between 20% to 49% in the standard questionnaire, while Platinum is awarded to buildings that achieve 90% and up.

While BOMA 360 has six categories of assessment, BOMA Best has 10: Energy, water, air, comfort, health and wellness, custodial, purchasing, waste, site, and stakeholder engagement.[4]

In 2021, certification fees for BOMA Best ranged anywhere from CA$2,670 for small healthcare facilities, up to CA$16,800 for non-member office buildings larger than two million square feet.[5] BOMA certifications last for three years and renewal comes with a fee.

BREEAM

The UK's BREEAM Certification is a sustainability assessment method for commercial and residential buildings, administered by BRE Global and offered globally.

BREEAM has nine categories on which a building and its ownership are graded: Energy, water, materials, pollution, land use and ecology, health and wellbeing, waste, transport, and management.

At the end of the assessment process, buildings receive a grade out of 100:

- Unclassified: > 10
- Acceptable: ≥ 10 to <25
- Pass: ≥ 25 to <40
- Good: ≥ 40 to <55

- Very Good: ≥ 55 to <70
- Excellent: ≥ 70 to <85
- Outstanding: ≥85

Certificates are valid for three years and cost £2,350 in total, with a renewal process that requires a fee of £190.[6]

ENERGY STAR

ENERGY STAR certification is administered in the United States by the U.S. Environmental Protection Agency and is awarded to buildings that achieve an ENERGY STAR score of 75 or higher, indicating that the building performs better than at least 75% of similar buildings nationwide based on a sample set of data.[7] It is free to apply, but building applications must be verified by a Professional Engineer or registered architect. This service typically costs $1,000 to $1,500 per site.[8]

Green Globes

The Green Building Initiative administers the Green Globes—an online assessment for Green building design, operations, and management. Green Globes offers three levels of certification: Certified, Gold, and Platinum. Building projects register for a fee of $1,500 to fill out a questionnaire online which has four broad categories: Sustainable management, social and economic factors, cultural heritage, and environmental.[9]

Questionnaire responses are reviewed and verified by a Green Globes assessor. The assessment incurs a fee that usually runs up to thousands of dollars. Banners, certificates, plaques, and window decals to promote the certification are individually available for purchase from GBI.[10]

LEED

And of course, one of the most pervasive Green certifications is LEED—Leadership in Energy and Environmental Design—administered by the U.S. Green Building Council's Green Business Certification Inc. (GBCI).

As we discussed in Chapter 1, LEED certification is based on a point system. Candidate buildings must prove certain prerequisites and minimum requirements to qualify for one of four levels of certification: Certified, Silver, Gold, and Platinum.

LEED now offers certification not just for building design and construction, but also building maintenance and operations, interior design and construction, homes, and neighborhood development.

For certification, buildings are assessed on their performance in nine criteria:

1 Sustainability
The building's ability to limit its impact on the ecology, environment and waterways around it

2 Water efficiency
Reducing water consumption and treating water efficiently and environmentally

3 Indoor environmental quality
The removal, diminishment, and control of sources of air pollution within the building, and well as providing a thermostat system control device to guarantee comfortable temperatures

4 Material and resources
Using building materials that leave less of an environmental impact, reducing and controlling waste, and decreasing the quantity of materials needed

5 Energy and atmosphere
Maximizing energy efficiency, using renewable and alternative energy sources, and adhering to ozone protection protocols

6 Location and transportation
Conserving green space and being environmentally sensitive by slowing urban sprawl and providing public transport access to the building

7 Innovation
Incorporating new technologies and using up-to-date scientific research in building design strategies

8 Regional priority
Being sensitive to the environmental issues particular to the building's locale

9 Education and Awareness
Providing building users—such as tenants or residential homeowners—with the necessary knowledge to run their systems properly. Publicly promoting green building and the LEED rating system.

Depending on the building type—residential, commercial, industrial, or multi-use—buildings must recertify every three or five years.

Since the total cost of a LEED certification is not traditionally publicly disclosed by either the certifiers or recipients of certification, it is difficult to find exact data on how much LEED certification truly costs. A 2010 court case revealed that LEED certification at the time cost a minimum of $2,900 for a new building under 50,000 square feet.[11] One study found that LEED certification for newly constructed buildings over 500,000 square feet incur total fees of around $20,000, and certification of one new hospital built in California in the 2000s exceeded $1 million.[12]

A 2015 study conducted by architects Berman Wright compared the certification of two similar newly constructed residence halls at the University of North Carolina, Charlotte. The first, Miltimore Hall, was a $32 million, 172,000 square feet project. The second, Belk Hall, was a $27 million, 168,000 square feet development. Miltimore Hall was LEED certified while Belk Hall was Green Globes certified. The total cost for LEED certification was $71,785, while the total cost for the Green Globes project was $29,425.[13] What is striking about the vast difference in costs for the two certification projects, according to the author of the study, is that the same assessment team performed both the LEED and the Green Globes assessments.

From the above descriptions of the six different organizations, there are two things to notice about the business of Green certification. The first is that each organization that offers a certification—whether it's the U.S. Green Building Council, BOMA, the Green Building Initiative, or the EPA—have articulated their own subjective view of what it means to be Green. Each organization measures materially different criteria. Even when the factors overlap, each organization has its own way of formulating their assessment of that criteria. There is no true common denominator among the many standards offered. The standards set by the organizations are not interchangeable.

A subjective view of what should be an objective reality

It is indisputable that the criteria for each of these certifications is important to measure. To varying degrees, the six organizations mentioned recognize the importance of sustainability in most of its forms. They exhibit a comprehensive understanding of the need to minimize the impact of buildings on the environment, the need to maximize social good, and the need for building developers and operators to exhibit good governance. These are all important goals for any building.

Through their individual certification programs, these organizations are articulating what they consider to be best practice in the development, management, and operation of Green buildings. These differences belie an important truth: Each organization has created different standards for what it means to be a "Green" building. If a building does not meet their particular definition of Green, then they will not certify it.

If different organizations claim to measure the same principle in different ways, then it follows that their criteria of measurement is subjective, rather than objective. Put another way, Green building certification companies take what should be an objective measure and make it highly subjective.

Not only are these standards materially different from each other, but because of the flexibility of the formulas used to certify buildings, the properties *that meet the same standard* can also be markedly different from one another.

Take BOMA 360, as an example. As we saw above, BOMA awards the most points for environmental and sustainability criteria—as it should. Buildings can achieve a maximum of 26 points in this category, but they only need a minimum of 12 for a passing grade. So, if one building scores 26 and another scores 12, both buildings can conceivably be certified in the same category. One wonders how a building with less than half the sustainability points can be deemed equal to another.

Such flexible criteria add an extra element of subjectivity into the mix. But why is subjectivity important? Because if a concept is described subjectively, it is considered an opinion rather than fact. If climate change and sustainability are portrayed as matters of opinion, this denies the objective fact of their existence and effects on the world.

Subjective, flexible criteria in Green building certifications exist for a very specific reason: They widen the pool of buildings that can be deemed certifiable, and therefore increase the revenue potential of the certification product.

That's all well and good if you are trying to market a product, but it might not be the most useful approach to sparking real and effective change. If Green certification is deemed a valuable commodity, then more companies will purchase it.

A broad reach is a useful tool to encourage buildings to "get with the program" on sustainability. And Green certifications have indeed been deemed a valuable commodity. The number of buildings certified throughout the world grows every year. If widespread purchasing of Green certification leads to an overall improvement in sustainability, then that is generally a good thing. But is it enough? I would argue it is not.

Take energy usage as an example of a flexible criterion within a Green building certification, and the implications of using subjective measures. Each organization—USGBC, BRE Group, BOMA, and the others—have an opinion regarding what level of energy usage is considered Green. Usually this is articulated as being "energy efficient" in some way or another, but the measures of energy efficiency can vary. A building can be deemed Green without, for example, being carbon neutral. Certainly, few certifications *require* a building to be energy regenerative. Should net zero and energy regeneration be the goal? Being energy regenerative is arguably the condition required to truly be a sustainable building.

It should also be noted that what is considered Green energy usage by certification shops in one part of the world might not be considered

Green in other parts of the world—for instance, the United States versus Europe, the Middle East, or Sub-Saharan Africa. So, even regionally among certification shops there are differences in what constitutes Green in one part of the world and what constitutes Green in another.

From a marketing perspective, regionality makes sense. Local markets in developing countries where there may be an appetite for a certification product might never be able to achieve the criteria levels of, for instance, LEED in the United States. So, just like McDonald's, the menu changes slightly from region to region to ensure the product is more palatable to the local population.

Of course, such differentiation also makes a certain amount of sense. Buildings can be built many different ways around the world. What's appropriate for an office building in San Diego may not be suitable for an office building in London, let alone Dubai or Nairobi. My argument here is not against regionality as such, merely to highlight the marketing imperative that exists if a commercial organization wishes to enter a new geography. But if establishing new criteria to suit a local market comes at the cost of objectivity and end results, the question must be asked: what is the value of the certification in the first place?

These regional differences also serve to underline the subjectivity of Green certification: Right from the start, the *Green* that was articulated by certification companies has always been malleable, depending on the audience. From the standpoint of Green certifications, *greenness* is always a moveable, debatable condition, depending on the circumstances in which it finds itself. Unfortunately, this means that its very premise—the very foundation of Green certification—stands on shaky ground. None of it is objective.

Course correction

Even certification providers themselves would understand and perhaps begrudgingly accept their subjectivity. Most of them—LEED, BOMA and BREEAM in particular—originated in architectural or design methodologies, articulating the perspectives of architects and engineers, specifically on the subject of what constituted Green practices in the construction and renovation of buildings.

The original certification model was all about the design specification of an asset. If developers or retrofitters could literally hit a checklist—and if they paid enough money—they would be awarded a plaque.

Later in the evolution of their products, certification providers started talking more about the operations of buildings.

You can imagine the conversation in the boardroom of Green certification companies.

Board Member 1: *"We are only concentrating on the buildings being constructed, yet at any single point in time, this is an incredibly small percentage of the overall built environment. So, why don't we develop a certification for how existing buildings are being used? That way, we can sell more certifications."*

Board Member 2: *"And we also stand a better chance of improving the sustainability of the built environment."*

Board Member 1: *"That too."*

The development of operational criteria—as worthy and appropriate as it may be—can still be seen effectively as certification providers admitting that their product fell short of achieving its stated goal: Improving the sustainability of the built environment. It is a recognition of their own weaknesses.

Consider the igloo. It consumes no energy. It's resource efficient. Its building materials are entirely natural and produced by hand. In its environment, it is purpose-built and resilient. In fact, it would be difficult to imagine a more environmentally perfect and sustainable structure. But show me an igloo that has been Green certified. I am not aware of the certification provider who has ever put a plaque on the door of an igloo. Without certification, is an igloo not Green?

Ultimately, Green standards and certifications are a payment system for plaques to affirm that a project was completed to someone's subjective opinion of Green. The notion that you need to pay a fee to certify that your building is Green is to accept the narrative perpetuated by certification providers. Shouldn't the data speak for itself? Isn't it really a question of measuring and monitoring the appropriate criteria?

Certifications cannot predict the future state of an asset

Taking a snapshot of a building's health at a given point in time serves many important purposes. It is a way of proving compliance with government regulations, such as energy usage and responsible waste disposal. It provides a method for marketing the building to prospective tenants and buyers. The assessment process for re-certification provides a set of forward-looking goals toward which an organization can strive. But certification does not provide a real-time— nor accurate or actionable—account of a building's health.

If a doctor tells you that you are healthy today, does that mean that you will remain healthy for the next three-to-five years? A doctor's examination and prognosis can only provide you with an accurate account of your health on that day. Any prognosis a doctor provides for your future health is based on statistics of likely risk, given your present health and other underlying conditions. A doctor's prognosis is probabilistic, not deterministic.

There is an interesting comparison to be made between how Green building certifications have historically been used, and how travelers were screened using Polymerase Chain Reaction (PCR) tests during the COVID-19 pandemic. Many airlines and governments required travelers to show proof of a negative PCR test result (i.e. proof that you had not contracted COVID) before they could board a flight or be admitted into a nation's borders. The test usually needed to be administered no more than 72 hours prior to admittance on the flight or to the country.

The policy served to help stem the spread of the disease, not because it caught every single case of a person traveling while suffering from COVID, but because it reduced the statistical likelihood of those people traveling. But the system was not foolproof. A negative test performed 72 hours ago does not mean that you do not have COVID at the time of travel. It simply means that up to three days ago, at the time you took the test, you did not have the virus.

In the context of COVID-19, a lot could happen in the three days since a potential traveler last had a PCR test. They could have contracted the virus from a family member, or even in a taxi on the way to the airport.

Similarly, in the context of sustainable building, a lot can happen in the three years since a property last had a Green certification.

Furthermore, although PCR tests were seen to be more accurate than other methods of testing—such as an antigen (otherwise known as "rapid") test—there was a statistically significant possibility of false negatives (by some measures for some tests, up to 29%).[14]

For the purposes of comparison between PCR tests and Green certification, the existence of false negatives can be articulated as follows: Just because your PCR test is negative, doesn't mean you don't have COVID, it simply means you are statistically less likely to have contracted the disease. By comparison, just because a certification provider has assessed a building as Green, doesn't mean it is necessarily a Green building.

Green buildings and dolphin-safe tuna fish

In March 2021, when a large portion of the world's population was still stuck indoors watching endless hours of television, Netflix released a film called *Seaspiracy*. The documentary purported to reveal the environmental impact of the fishing industry. The film followed the supply chain of the commercial seafood industry and questioned the validity of sustainable seafood certifications.

In particular, the film criticizes the Dolphin Safe label given to certain canned tuna brands. At one point in the documentary, British filmmaker Ali Tabrizi speaks with Mark Palmer, associate U.S. director of the International Marine Mammal Project, the organization responsible for the Dolphin Safe certification. Tabrizi asks Palmer if the IMMP could guarantee that no dolphin was ever killed in the fishing of Dolphin Safe-labelled tuna. Palmer answers: "no."

Further discussions reveal that there are no assurances that just because a participant measures up to certification standards on one day, it does not mean that they might not accidentally kill a dolphin in the future.

It is not hard to draw comparisons to any purported certification—including Green building. A positive result at one particular point in time does not preclude a negative result down the line.

In the case of Dolphin Safe tuna, Palmer has since accused the filmmakers of misrepresenting his views.

"I answered [that] there are no guarantees in life but that drastically reducing the number of vessels intentionally chasing and netting dolphins as well as other regulations in place, that the number of dolphins that are killed is very low," Palmer told the Guardian newspaper.[15]

A spokesperson for another sustainable fishing certification provider, the Marine Stewardship Council, said that to say there is no such thing as sustainable fishing—and that by implication the MSC certification was not credible—was misleading.

"Some of the known problems that the film highlights—bycatch, overfishing, and destruction of marine ecosystems—are precisely the issues the MSC certification process is designed to address," a spokesperson said.

In response, Tabrizi told the newspaper: "[Credible marine scientists] expose the failure of sustainable fishing in the film, [and] explain how the term 'sustainable' is so vague that even bycatch of seabirds, dolphins, and seals can be considered sustainable. This is not what consumers think of when they pick up a filet of fish with the MSC blue tick."

Of Palmer's complaint about being supposedly misquoted, Tabrizi went on to say:

"We did not claim … the Dolphin Safe label is a conspiracy … We asked if they could guarantee 'Dolphin Safe' tuna is in fact dolphin safe, to which Mark Palmer replied that they could not … The label does not say 95% dolphin safe. It claims to be dolphin safe. In the words of Mark Palmer himself, 'one dolphin and you're out'. This wasn't taken out of context."

You can imagine a similar conversation between Green certification providers and their detractors.

How can the market know that when a provider certifies a building as Green, that the provider is monitoring the building's compliance over the long haul and ensuring that it remains sustainable between certifications?

Without objective, independent data, the market cannot know this.

The providers of Dolphin Safe certification counter with an argument that could easily be adapted to the Green building certification business. Their retort to the Seaspiracy filmmakers can be paraphrased as follows:

The Dolphin Safe tuna certification has led to the largest decline in dolphin deaths by tuna fishing in history. Without the certification and education program, hundreds of thousands more dolphins would die. The program is important to helping support ocean biodiversity. Fishing companies that go through an assessment work hard to reach the standards set.

This argument bears serious consideration. Has the program helped protect dolphins and marine ecology? On balance, the answer is undoubtedly yes. And that protection is a valuable proposition. But has the program saved dolphins from eventual extinction and stopped the fishing industry from irreparably harming the marine ecology? While it is too early to say definitively one way or another, it is extremely unlikely that Dolphin Safe certification alone will save dolphins from human harm.

As Callum Roberts, a marine conservationist at the University of Exeter, puts it: "My colleagues may rue the statistics, but the basic thrust of it is we are doing a huge amount of damage to the ocean and that's true. At some point you run out. Whether it's 2048 or 2079, the question is: 'Is the trajectory in the wrong direction or the right direction?'"

Surely the same can be said of Green building certifications. As a society, we are doing extreme damage to the environment. Green certifications have helped draw attention to the role in which the built environment can induce or mitigate this harm. But we are at a point where the harm needs to be measured and monitored on an ongoing basis. What is required of us to mitigate this damage is not a static certification updated every few years.

Assets aren't sustainable or unsustainable. They exist on a spectrum as data points that can be measured consistently. Buildings can change. The least sustainable building can improve, and the most sustainable building can degrade.

The idea that buildings can only be Green if they are made with the newest sustainable building materials using the most innovative, cutting-edge technologies—a gleaming tower built with net zero emissions—ignores the billions of buildings that already exist. What is arguably more important than grading new buildings is improving pre-existing buildings—whether they be 1960s tower blocks or medieval cathedrals, it is how the building is being run that is ultimately important.

Lessons from the bond ratings market

Like many certification programs, a regime of paying people to provide a platinum plaque—a piece of marketing collateral—serves only the interests of the certification providers and the real estate owners. It does little to serve the interests of investors.

The makers of certifications want to design a product that the market will accept. And they need wide acceptance if they are to make money from their standard. Quite obviously, certification providers are building a product to sell to real estate owners—a product designed to have marketing cachet. In turn, real estate owners will be induced to purchase that product because if the certification gains wide acceptance, it will be useful for marketing to tenants. But to ensure wide acceptance of a certification regime—and therefore to maximize profitability—the process and requirements of certification cannot be overly burdensome or expensive, or else it would put off potential new customers.

There is another model of pay-to-play assessment that resembles Green certification: The bond ratings market.

Government and corporate bonds are rated by credit agencies—notably Standard & Poor's, Moody's, and Fitch.

Bond ratings provide a useful measure for comparing securities. Credit ratings agencies rate bonds based on the financial strengths, prospects, and past history of the issuer. Entities—whether they be companies, nations, states, or even municipalities—that are financially sound—with manageable levels of debt, good debt-paying records, and good earnings potential—have good credit ratings. Entities deficient in those criteria don't. Bonds with good credit ratings are believed to have a lower risk of default. Institutional investors generally adhere to a policy of limiting bond investments to only "investment-grade" (i.e. high quality) bonds due to their historically low default rates. Ergo, the better the credit rating, the more likely a bond will be attractive to investors.

Like Green certifications, credit ratings agencies are a pay-to-play model; companies or governments that wish to issue debt pay the credit agency to evaluate and assess the company or government and the debt instrument, and subsequently provide a credit worthiness report.

Unlike Green certifications, credit ratings agencies review their individual bond ratings frequently—usually quarterly, as to provide a regular assessment of a bond's creditworthiness. They do not rate a bond and then forget about it for three to five years.

To make their calculations and assessment, bond ratings use systematic, quantitative analysis based on hard financial data and a standardized approach, so that all bonds can be compared against the same criteria. It is an apples-to-apples approach to measurement.

Bond rating agencies are regulated by the government. They are subject to strict rules and enforcement regarding the consistency and honesty of their ratings and the transparency of their assessment criteria.

Participation from issuing entities is mandatory. Bond ratings are not voluntary. If an entity wishes to issue a bond, it must undergo assessment by a credit ratings agency. Results are published regularly so that the market has timely information on which to react. If an issuer receives a bad rating, they have little alternative but to improve their financial performance and creditworthiness or face the label of 'junk bond.'

These last two features of bond ratings providers sit in stark contrast to Green building certification providers. There is no specific regulatory oversight of Green building certification providers other than the rules against fraud and negligence under which all businesses operate. There is no requirement for certification providers to be transparent about their criteria or assessment. And Green certification certainly is not mandatory for all property developers or operators who participate in the market. It is a voluntary election.

Of course, the bond ratings market is not without its challenges or missteps. In the global financial crisis of 2008-09, these organizations were heavily criticized for their inability to identify faults in the creditworthiness of mortgage-backed securities and subprime mortgage bond issuers. The U.S. government's Financial Crisis Inquiry Commission found that credit agency "failures" were "key enablers of the financial meltdown," specifically because they did not properly perform their job of evaluating the creditworthiness of mortgage-backed security issuers.[16]

In the aftermath of the global financial crisis, the SEC created an Office of Credit Ratings charged with monitoring the activities and conducting examinations of these organizations to assess and promote compliance with statutory and SEC requirements.

Of prime importance to the SEC and U.S. government is the relationship between paying for ratings and the assessment of the resulting grade. In a report to Congress on the credit rating agencies' part in the global financial crisis, the SEC pointed out several conflicts of interest inherent in the issuer-pay model. The first was what the SEC called "rating shopping"—the practice of bond issuers engaging multiple credit rating agencies to analyze their bond, and then going with whatever agency provides the best rating. Another conflict was that companies that offer a large volume of bonds might be able to "exert greater undue influence" on a credit agency to obtain better ratings, because the agency may fear losing their business.[17]

The SEC has since sought to modify the regulation of credit agencies to minimize the risk of such adverse market forces. While there is still work to do, the observations that the SEC and other experts have made of the credit ratings market may be useful to observers of the Green building certification market. There is no reason to believe these market dynamics could not be at play in the Green certification business.

Green building certifications are not a regulated market. They are not law. And if they are subjective, how can they possibly be considered science?

Introducing data and transparency into the mix

GRESB—formerly the Global Real Estate Sustainability Benchmark—provides an industry standard for real estate investments at the portfolio level. The benchmark is notable for its use of ESG metrics to capture information regarding ESG performance and sustainability.

In 2020, GRESB charged an "assessment participation fee" of $4,800 for every submission. The fee for organizations with many participating portfolios was capped at $43,200.[18] That fee provides participants with guidance materials and helpdesk support, and includes access to a benchmark report, data exporter, and portfolio analysis tool. The portfolio analysis tool allows users to perform analyses such as:

- Measure ESG performance against a self-selected benchmark
- Calculate the environmental footprint of a portfolio
- Identify the investments leading and lagging on ESG performance
- Calculate the portfolio's environmental efficiency in terms of energy consumption, greenhouse emissions, water usage, and waste.

GRESB arguably stands alone in the Green building certification and assessment market for its embrace of hard data and its refusal to offer any form of certification. Instead, GRESB takes the approach of providing material information on assets at the portfolio level. Taking a cue from the accounting profession's reliance and presentation of financial data, GRESB gives each reporter a score and provides ESG data reports. In short, it provides data, not certifications, and purports to use transparent, objective criteria to help portfolio managers assess the sustainability of their real estate assets.

As evolutionary as this approach is, the same flaws transpire with the GRESB model as with Green building certification models. Even GRESB's model is based on an annual benchmark and report, capturing a moment in time rather than the real-time, everyday performance of an asset. It also has an element of subjectivity.

Essentially, GRESB has determined a Green portfolio must have a defined level for each ESG criteria—for instance, energy efficiency—adding an element of opinion into the final product.

Portfolio managers, it should be noted, need to pay GRESB to provide them with a report. The reports are not free.

Built-to-sell or built-to-solve?

Built-to-Sell certifications that are designed for the purpose of marketing buildings based on point-in-time assessments and subjective opinions, will not solve the problem of climate change. Given their intrinsic nature, it is hard to imagine such a system gaining enough momentum and effecting enough environmental change to improve the planet's situation. And real estate needs to be a big part of the solution to climate change. The built environment—residential, commercial, and industrial real estate—is the cause of 40% of carbon emissions. As much as certification providers would delight in the proposition, every building on the planet cannot possibly be certified Green. Yet every building on the planet needs to be part of the solution and help reduce carbon emissions.

Reducing society's reliance on carbon-based fuels is an imperative for businesses and governments alike. The European Union's 2030 Climate Target Plan aims to reduce greenhouse gas emissions to at least 55% below 1990 levels by the end of the decade. In the United States, the Biden administration's goal is to cut the country's emissions at least 50% by 2030. These are ambitious targets that will not be solved by a certification model.

Rather than concentrating on certifying a number of buildings as shades of Green, the real estate industry needs to be measuring the carbon emissions of all buildings and implementing target reductions based on science.

The world's needs have moved on from what Green certification can offer. The business of building certifications is not about decarbonization. It is about selling certifications. Certifications may well have at their core a desire to save the planet. But when you depart from objective, science-based assessments of what needs to be done for the world, and you move toward subjective criteria for what can be reasonably sold to a market of property owners, then you will naturally need to make accommodations to your original proposition.

There is nothing wrong with wanting to sell real estate asset owners Green building certifications. And there is nothing wrong with real estate asset owners wanting to buy Green building certifications so that they can market their Green credentials to potential tenants and buyers. But it is wrong for the real estate industry to rely solely on Green certifications as a tool to genuinely improve sustainability. It will not work.

A tool to genuinely improve sustainability

Earlier on, we talked about what real estate buyers need to make informed decisions about purchasing an asset. What they needed was accurate data: Data about the location of the property, data about the valuation of the property, and data about the property's ability to match the needs of the buyer.

Buyers expect this data to be accurate and standardized. When they want to understand a rental property's income potential, they analyze its rental income. When brokers conduct a valuation of a property for sale, they look at comparable properties to determine the listing price. Although they take Green building certification into consideration, brokers do not buy and sell buildings based purely on a claim of certification. A platinum building does not equal a specific square-foot value. Buyers and sellers alike form their own opinion based on their reading of data.

Rather than focus on doling out Green certifications, should we not simply provide the market with ESG data and let participants decide if a building's performance is Green enough for them? When the data is freely available, the certification ceases to have utility.

Once upon a time the market would not have been able to cope with raw ESG data—nor would it have even wanted such data. Until recently, there was no consensus over what metrics mattered when comparing two buildings in terms of sustainability. However, thanks in large part to the work of Green building certification and assessment companies like BREEAM, LEED, and GRESB, real estate professionals and investors are now closer to having a working framework from which they can make decisions. Green building certifications helped cultivate and formalize the real estate sustainability conversation. They gave it substance and structure. Without certification companies, we would not have seen the evolution from the Green of the 1960s to the ESG of today.

But now that we have arrived in the ESG era, certifications have served their purpose, and we do not need them anymore. The market no longer needs voluntary annual reports. It just needs the data.

We are now at a point in time where real estate professionals can analyze ESG data and form their own opinions. Asset owners and investors no longer need to pay a third party to do the analysis and assessment for them. All they need is access to the data. The data doesn't need to be certified anymore. It just needs to be measured.

Even Green building organizations themselves have begun to acknowledge this fact. In their first iteration, certification providers supplied a single point-in-time certification, essentially indicating that once a building was certified Green—based on its design and construction—it was Green forever. Next came the evolution to certifying a building periodically based on its actual performance. Periodical certification is a promising development, but it does not go far enough. Taken to its logical conclusion, it is a recognition that a building's ESG performance should be measured continuously.

There is no such thing as 'Green' or 'not Green.' There is only the context of when the building was constructed and how it is currently being operated. And context can only be determined by continual measurement.

Energy efficiency is a good case in point. There is no doubt that energy efficiency is important for every building. But it becomes critically important for high energy consuming operations such as server farms and factories. If a business is not a high energy consuming operation, then it might not need to invest as much into the energy efficiency of its offices. A business that consumes small quantities of energy in an inefficient building may be able to lower its carbon footprint better than a high energy consuming business in an energy efficient building. Or the businesses may emit the same total amount of carbon. Energy efficiency—and by association greenness—is not a matter of being a box to tick on a certification checklist. It is a spectrum to be measured on a continuous basis.

If you are measuring your calorie intake for a diet, you don't want to know that a sandwich has somewhere between 600 and 1,500 calories. You want to know precisely how many calories that sandwich has. If you are buying a used car, it is not enough just to know that the car's odometer reads somewhere between 1,000 miles and 100,000 miles. Buyers want to know exactly how many miles the car has been driven.

Consumers expect accurate data to help them make their decisions. The modern consumer has a nuanced understanding of data. The more gradients of data they have, the better they can match their needs with a product.

Chapter 4:
The Rise of Regulation

The real estate industry is moving away from Green certifications and toward government-mandated disclosure of actual reporting data. This move is happening because the market is no longer satisfied with voluntary frameworks that are opaque and inadequate for making investment decisions. In this new environment, objectivity and robust data will be the top priority for all market participants—builders, building managers, asset owners, investors, and tenants alike.

A tale of two regulations

When it comes to the development of regulatory frameworks, there are two competing models: top-down and bottom-up. In a top-down system, regulations are developed at a national or regional level and handed down to lower levels of government (such as states and municipalities) for enactment, monitoring, and enforcement. The nature of the regulation in Europe—which is also becoming the dominant philosophy in Australasia—is a top-down approach. In bottom-up systems, regulations are created at the local level and permeate upwards. Bottom-up regulatory systems are usually characteristic of federal systems such as the United States.

In the U.S. especially, the codification of building and development laws often starts at the municipal level and then spreads to the states. Overlaid across this labyrinth of local and state codes are Federal statutes that exist as an umbrella of standards.

Municipalities—and even states—often do not agree with each other in terms of what they prohibit in building construction or energy usage, or even how they implement Federal law.

Building permits—the authorization for construction of a new building or renovation of an existing building—are handled by the local government. These permits require design and construction of a new building or renovation to adhere to local and state laws. But while many of these local regulations are based on the national model codes we covered earlier, not all municipalities or states adopt the codes, let alone the latest version of these model codes. The result is a patchwork of rules that require would-be developers to understand a multitude of local laws when entering a new market. Further still, code adoption does not necessarily mean code enforcement, and many municipalities and states do not have either the resources or the inclination to ensure buildings are up to code.[1]

Patchwork rules are a real problem for developers in the United States. Disparate rules between different cities require extra planning and cost. If all local governments in America used and enforced the most current model codes developed by the Federal government, then there would be more consistency across the United States.

Differing rules also impede the real estate industry's ability to combat the impact of climate change. When different jurisdictions across the country impose inconsistent rules on carbon emissions, water usage, and energy efficiency, real estate developers and owners must bear the cost of multiple compliance systems and significant uncertainty from market to market. Consistency is what is needed if the country is to contribute as a nation to reducing the risks of climate change.

European regulations, on the other hand, provide an example of a top-down regulatory framework. Rules are handed down from Brussels after extensive research and deliberation over what must be the standard across the EU. Laws are then propagated to Member States, either as regulations or directives, for those countries to promulgate, implement, and enforce. The standardization that comes from a top-down approach provides for a more efficient and cost-effective compliance system as well as a high level of certainty.

The American system is a product of how highly the nation prizes individuality, libertarianism, and trust in the market to regulate the economy. The European experience, alternately, rose out of a belief that European nations needed to cooperate to solve the region's problems. A central government body—presumably after extensive research and consultation—determines the measures that are important for society as a whole, and requires all levels of government, businesses, and citizens to adhere to those common requirements.

In the realm of building codes, uniformity means that developers can better plan their compliance across multiple projects and jurisdictions, and they can benefit from more cost savings on materials. In turn, real estate users can be sure to enjoy a more uniform offering.

Bottom-up and top-down regulatory models also have their impact on those investing in real estate. As we have already established, the U.S. financial regulator—the SEC—now requires all listed companies to disclose ESG information. Yet it does not prescribe a framework for that disclosure. The result is a patchwork of different types of disclosures that often do not bear much resemblance from company to company. The EU, on the other hand, has a detailed framework for sustainability reporting. We will cover these differences more in the following sections, but despite their differences—and failings—these two types of regulatory models nonetheless have a common thread. As different as these two types of lawmaking are, they both seem to be leading to the same place: The rise of sustainability regulation and the enshrining of ESG principles into law.

Readers may have already noticed that one of the themes of this book is the notion that non-financial data—especially ESG data—is rising in esteem and parity to traditional financial variables, such as assets, cash flow, expenses, equity, income, and liabilities. The reason for this development is simple: If data is material to a real estate investment decision, then it needs to be documented and reported in a standardized manner. Otherwise, investors do not have the full story and can therefore not make considered decisions. Until recently, the market did not consider ESG factors as material. And while some people might still think that ESG's materiality is not quite on par with traditional financial variables, the signs are pointing towards a time when ESG data as material will be the prevailing view.

The reason is simple: When an activity is not regulated, it cannot be guaranteed that the people performing that activity will abide by the same set of rules. In times when that activity is not deemed to be important, such differences rarely matter much to those engaged in the activity, nor to society as a whole. Manners and common courtesy are a good example. It's nice to have pleasant manners, and people with good manners are rewarded for their courteous behavior. But we do not jail people for rudeness.

And there was a time when building sustainably was seen as a good thing to do—but not critical to be a successful real estate developer. In that time, Green certification was seen as a good thing to do, but it was not a necessity. Yet as society has come to realize the increasing detrimental impact of global climate change, the importance of sustainable building has begun to be seen as an imperative. As a result, market participants around the world—coming from different political, cultural, and jurisprudential systems—are arriving at the same conclusion: Voluntary reporting will not change behaviors enough to improve the wholesale state of the built environment, nor will it affect the change necessary to combat the climate crisis.

The market—and market participants from investors to tenants—are increasingly voicing their frustration over poor building practices and developers ignoring sustainability. There has recently been a wholesale societal shift that is moving the real estate industry towards improved behavior. It is a trend that echoes a similar industry transformation that happened over a century ago.

Lessons from America's food crisis

In the late 1800s, the quality and availability of fresh food was distinctly lacking in the United States. The country was in a sharp phase of urbanization, and many rural dwellers were moving to the big cities in search of employment. Yet this rural flight only served to exacerbate strains in the nation's food supply chain. Much of the vegetables and meat consumed by this growing urban population was what today we would consider rotten and far beyond human consumption. As a result, Americans were dying as a direct consequence of eating poorly prepared, stored—and sometimes intentionally poisonous—foods.

In 1906, author Upton Sinclair wrote his novel *The Jungle*, detailing the dire conditions and poor practices at a Chicago meatpacking plant. In a bid to cut costs and meet skyrocketing demand, rotten meat was intentionally ground up with poisoned rats, then canned and sold to consumers as processed beef. The book captured the nation's attention, and the public outcry was palpable. *The Jungle* had touched a nerve, and soon more stories of an industry free of regulation and rampant with bad practices were revealed.

In a speech to Congress on June 21 that same year, Representative James Mann of Illinois famously produced a plate of so-called fresh cherries and explained how they had been adulterated to be marketed to the public. Originally picked green but then drained of color with acid to keep them firm, the cherries were then recolored red with poisonous aniline dye.[2]

Meatpackers and butchers regularly used toxic boric acid to preserve meat and red dye to give the appearance of freshness. Liquor makers often used poisonous chemicals in the distillation of whiskey. Soon the U.S. government was forced to address the appalling conditions in the unregulated food market.

The result was the 1906 Pure Food and Drug Act, which set down standards for food production, distribution, and storage. The new law also called for the prohibition of false and misleading statements about ingredients. The act established a national regulator which was eventually to become the U.S. Food and Drug Administration.

Over the next 60 years, new laws were added to protect the health of citizens. In 1912, after an outcry over a sleeping tonic for babies which was found to contain morphine and guaranteed a "good night's sleep" for babies and their mothers, the act was amended to prohibit false therapeutic claims on drugs.

In 1962, after Thalidomide—used in sleeping pills in Western Europe—was identified as the cause of birth defects, the FDA began requiring that drug manufacturers prove by scientific method that their products were effective, before they would be permitted to market them.

The regulatory framework that the U.S. government established was an evidence-based system. Before a product could be put on the market, its manufacturers and distributors had to prove to the FDA that their product not only did what it promised, but also that it would not cause harm. The government did not establish a voluntary system of self-certification. Instead, it determined that quantifiable scientific data needed to be the benchmark for whether a product was safe. Once these laws were promulgated and enforceable, overnight the government had the authority to sanction food and drug manufacturers for producing poisonous products or for making false advertising claims. The result has been a marked improvement in the quality of food and drugs in the American market, and by extension, the health of the American people.

But imagine, for a moment, that the FDA did not go down the path of regulating the market, requiring scientific data of claims, and punishing bad actors. Instead, it simply allowed independent, for-profit businesses to market a voluntary certification for the safety of food and drugs, using whatever criteria the certifiers saw fit and not requiring that data to be made public.

A new drug—let's say aspirin—might claim to cure headaches. Its manufacturer would pay the certification company to evaluate those claims and provide an assessment and a rating based on the assessment. Perhaps the rating system consisted of four levels: "Platinum," if the product cured headaches 100% of the time; "Gold," if the product was effective 50% of the time; "Silver" if the drug worked only on certain members of the population, but had extreme side-effects; or "Certified," if the drug seemed to work occasionally, but the data could not determine when or why it would be effective. My guess is that three things would happen:

1. The certification company would make itself a lot of money

2. Every drug manufacturer that *wanted* their drug certified *would* be able to obtain a certification at one level or another—whether the drug was effective against headaches or not
3. Pharmaceutical companies would be incentivized to concentrate on marketing their certification more than they would be incentivized to actually develop an effective drug

Perhaps you saw through my cunningly opaque headache analogy and immediately identified my true target?

Green building certifications were instrumental in raising awareness of the environmental and sustainability issues we face as a society, just like James Mann's 1906 cherry speech raised awareness of the dangers of adulterated foods. But in the same way that the logical next step in the problem of rotten food was the Pure Food Act, the logical next step for the building industry is the regulation of sustainability, based on concrete data. Without this next step, we simply will not meet the challenges we currently face.

The real estate industry must move away from Green certifications and towards consistent regulated frameworks and enforceable penalties for behavior that does not adhere to the principles of sustainability. If Green certifications do not move out of the way of progress, then they will become part of the problem and counterproductive to the issues we face as a business, and as a society. At this current point in time, with the issues that we face from intensifying climate change, a fixation on Green certifications is no less than willful ignorance of what is needed to improve the sustainability of the built environment. Under such conditions, Green certification is tantamount to greenwashing. Something must be done. The status quo cannot hold.

Some of the greatest luminaries of the Green building certification movement acknowledge that certifications will not lead to effective widespread change.

Engineer Jerry Yudelson, who *Wired Magazine* dubbed in 2011 the "Godfather of Green[3]," had been building solar houses for over a decade before LEED certifications were launched. Yudelson is a LEED Fellow and a former president of the Green Building Initiative, which created the Green Globes certification. For five years he was a board member of the U.S. Green Building Council. Yudelson thinks certifications are broken.

"The Green building revolution has failed to fulfill its promise to transform the marketplace in a meaningful way," Yudelson wrote in 2016. The reason, he believed, was simple. It was a matter of math. By 2015, less than one percent of commercial buildings and homes in the U.S. were LEED certified, yet the country was aiming to achieve a 50% reduction in carbon emissions by 2030. Green certifications, Yudelson argued, were not moving the needle.[4] Half a decade later, progress is no further along. CBRE's 2019 Green Building Adoption Index (the most recent iteration, at time of writing) showed that the percentage of commercial buildings that were LEED certified had actually dropped from 5.3% the year prior, to 5.1%.[5]

Yudelson says Green certification adoption has flatlined, rendering it toothless against rising carbon emissions. I believe that a large part of the reason for this flatline is that it has become obvious to the market that Green certification is not useful anymore. It is not an accurate method for judging the performance of a building, nor is it a robust framework to benchmark Green certified buildings against the wider market.

Tariq Fancy, the former CIO of BlackRock's sustainability funds, laid the situation out more bluntly for *The Guardian* in March 2021: "In many cases it's cheaper and easier to market yourself as Green rather than do the long tail work of actually improving your sustainability profile. [Doing the work to become sustainable is] expensive and if there is no penalty from the government, in the form of a carbon tax or anything else, then this market failure is going to persist."[6]

While Fancy was talking about greenwashing across all sectors of the market, he just as easily could have been talking specifically about the real estate sector. Fancy, and a number of other experienced institutional investors, had identified a trend that applies as much to

Green building certifications as it does elements of the fund management industry—something he termed "sustaina-babble."

Instead of creating investments geared towards actual climate impact, Fancy and others realized that fund managers were simply creating products to market to investors who were interested in ESG. As a result, in 2020, Fancy and others began pushing for more aggressive government policies and regulations to address environmental and societal problems.[7]

Kenneth Pucker, a professor at The Fletcher School at Tufts University, put it another way in a May-June *Harvard Business Review* article: "We're confusing output with impact."[8]

His basic argument was that the reporting and measuring of sustainability and ESG metrics is useless unless those measures are uniform, audited, and enforced by government regulation.

These ideas are taking hold, but not only in the ivory towers of investment banks and the boardrooms of real estate development companies. They are also taking root with everyday people—tenants of residential complexes, factory workers, and office workers who spend their days in downtown towers. These everyday folk increasingly do not care about the brand of the certification plaque on the wall. What they care about is whether the building they are inhabiting is actually sustainable.

The needs of the many

In the early 1900s, society stopped tolerating rotten food and false advertising in medicine, because otherwise it would not have survived. Investors do not tolerate adulterated or false financial information in the markets, because it impedes the proper functioning of the markets. It stands to reason that as ESG metrics become crucial, investors will not tolerate unscientific, inaccurate, or intentionally false information on sustainability either. The information an investor can glean from a Green certification is not comparable to other certifications, and it is not ubiquitous in the market, so it is severely limiting in its ability to inform the decision-making process. The arc to regulation is obvious.

I hasten to add, that I do not come to this conclusion from any philosophical position. This book is not a treatise on the merits or failings of any particular dogma. Staunch libertarians would no doubt argue that the government has no place in regulating food and drug markets. They would say businesses should be permitted to do and market whatever they wish to individuals who have free choice; let the market regulate bad actors out of existence and *caveat emptor*—let the buyer beware.

On the other end of the spectrum, hardline progressives might argue that for the good of society, the FDA should do more than just prohibit poisonous, falsely marketed, or unproved products. Instead, it should even prohibit products that are not actively good for you—like sugar or alcohol. I am not a philosopher. At their extremes, both viewpoints fall on to rather shaky ground. I put my faith in data, and its ability to provide an objective view and actionable information to make informed decisions.

This book also is not a damning critique of capitalism, or the effectiveness of market-based systems. Quite the opposite. I believe strongly in the capital markets and their ability to regulate price, supply, and demand. But for markets to work perfectly, they need perfect information—or as close to perfect as you can get.

Yet I can see how advocating for more regulation may seem counterintuitive to a pro-market view. But I believe that market participants actually desire a more robust regulatory regime for sustainability. It is alluringly easy to construct a conflict between business interests on the one hand and government on the other. Businesses, so the story goes, hate regulation because they object to limits on their ability to make money. Governments, apparently, are more interested in their own self-perpetuation. It certainly makes sense that businesses would resist restrictions on their growth and the increased costs that come with regulatory burden. And it may well be true that some developers and asset owners take this view. After all, the real estate industry is not a monolith. All real estate professionals do not think the same way.

Yet I do not believe this narrative is entirely true when it comes to the evolving regulatory environment in sustainability. Scratch a little deeper and you see that the market is the main driver in the trend to increased regulations and greater transparency on ESG and sustainability compliance.

In the United States in particular, where local and state building codes can vary widely, the prevailing view among developers and asset owners is that consistency would be favored over the need to navigate a patchwork of rules. Day-to-day, on building sites and in board rooms, developers have far fewer conversations about the merits of Green certification than they do about the latest rules and building codes that have sprung up in the jurisdictions in which they operate. It is a burden on their resources and checkbooks for real estate owners to have to keep up with all the different codes around the country. "Give me one rule that I know and can follow," they seem to be saying.

The market participants that matter the most—the buyers and tenants—are also calling for transparency of ESG information and government enforcement of bad actors.

In 2021, there was no more poignant and tragic example of the need for a refocus of building codes than the collapse of a residential building in Surfside, Florida. In June of that year, Champlain Towers South, a condominium just north of Miami Beach, collapsed, killing 98 people. The building had been inspected 177 times between January 2018 and August 2019, yet none of those inspections raised red flags about the building's severe structural damage.

Why?

As CNN put it in a report at the time, the inspectors' jobs were to ensure compliance with permits such as plumbing upgrades, air conditioning repairs, and window installations in individual units. They likely regularly walked past severe structural damage and ignored it, because they were not there to review the structure of the building. In the aftermath, wrote CNN, state and local officials around Florida were questioning whether periodic, structural inspections of buildings should become mandatory statewide, and what role government inspectors should play.[9]

Regardless of political leanings or philosophical preferences, two things seem clear to me:

1. Unless something is measured and monitored, it cannot be appraised. But at the same time:
2. Unless that appraisal leads to real change—in the form of improvements or sanctions against those who fail to act—then those appraisals are worthless.

The tragedy in Florida serves not only as a warning about the repercussions of neglect to an individual building, but also what can happen to our combined built environment if it is not monitored properly. Data needs to be not only measured and reported, but also used to improve, and enforce bad actors to change. If you believe in a particular political solution or philosophical explanation, back it up with real world data. And as it has been discussed previously, this is a view that seems to be increasingly shared by the market.

The regulators, as always, may have been slow to catch up with the views of society. But they are quickly heading to the same conclusion.

Regulations are catching up

On July 14, 2021, the European Commission proposed that the EU require Member States to renovate at least 3% of the total floor area of all public buildings annually—an increase in the current 1% requirement. The new rules are intended to improve energy efficiency and the sustainability of the bloc's built environment. In addition to residential buildings, public buildings must also be renovated to use more renewable energy, and to be more energy efficient.

To help fund these new requirements, and to kick-start the continent's redevelopment after the global Coronavirus pandemic, a new Social Climate Fund was established to support EU citizens most affected or at risk of energy poverty by mitigating the costs of redevelopment. The fund will provide €72.2 billion in funding over seven years for the renovation of buildings, and other activities.

The Commission also proposed setting a benchmark of 49% of renewables in buildings by 2030 and to require Member States to increase the use of renewable energy in heating and cooling by +1.1 percentage points each year, until 2030.

As discussed in Chapter 2, the EU's top-down regulation—in the form of targets and sanctions for those who do not meet the targets—also establishes criteria for sustainability disclosure of investment funds. On March 10, 2021, the EU's Sustainable Finance Disclosure Regulation (SFDR) became effective. The directive imposes sustainability-related disclosure requirements on banks, insurance companies, investment firms, and pension funds. These institutional investors must now be transparent about:

- How much sustainability risk assessment is integrated into their decision-making and due diligence
- How adverse sustainability impacts their investments
- The overall sustainability of their financial products

As we saw in Chapter 1, while not currently prescribing a specific format for how to disclose, the SEC nonetheless requires companies to disclose sustainability information. Several standard frameworks are available to use, including the Sustainability Accounting Standards Board and the Task Force on Climate-related Financial Disclosures.[10] But the securities watchdog has recently gone one step further in its views on sustainability reporting compliance. In mid-2021, the SEC proposed enhancing its corporate ESG disclosures rules, and part of that enhancement is aggressive enforcement. In July, the securities watchdog's Asset Management Advisory Committee advised the SEC to take steps to foster "meaningful, consistent, and comparable disclosure of material [ESG] matters by issuers" and provide an explanation if no disclosure framework is adopted.[11] The SEC has warned companies that it will increase enforcement of ESG disclosures, pursuing with stiff penalties those companies found to be opaque or misleading in their sustainability reports.[12]

In the EU, the U.S., and around the world, regulation is replacing voluntary approaches. The rise of regulation—whether bottom-up or top-down—is winning.

Business conversations in the real estate industry are not about being panicked over the latest version of LEED. Instead, they are about concern over new local building codes or fears of fines for noncompliance. Regulation is the real estate professional's benchmark, not Green certification. The rules over energy usage and carbon emissions set by the government are their goalposts, not whether their plaque is platinum, gold, or silver, because a shiny plaque bears no weight when the regulator comes knocking on your door. Developers and asset owners cannot say to an accusing regulator: "I know I didn't hit your emission targets, but I am Green certified by other metrics, so do I get a pass?"

Moving closer to uniformity, transparency, and objectivity

The evolution from Green certification to sustainability regulation has not happened accidentally. Instead, it has happened—and is accelerating—because of market forces. One of my core beliefs, which I have expressed throughout this book, is a faith in data as the fuel that drives the markets. The better the accuracy, transparency, and efficiency of the data, the better the market can function.

I believe that one of the drivers of the growing demand for increased sustainability regulation is the market's desire for more accurate, transparent, and efficient data. Why? Because the market requires material information that can be acted upon. Because the market wants to understand the risk associated with individual companies and funds. Because the market wants objective assurances that companies are meeting their commitments to combating climate change.

The chart below plots the information that can be derived from the various types of reporting frameworks available to investors looking to invest in real estate opportunities. On the Y axis is the uniformity and transparency of data, and on the X axis is its objectivity. A third line represents how actionable the information derived from a reporting framework is for market participants.

Uniformity, transparency, and objectiveness of information derived from real estate reporting frameworks

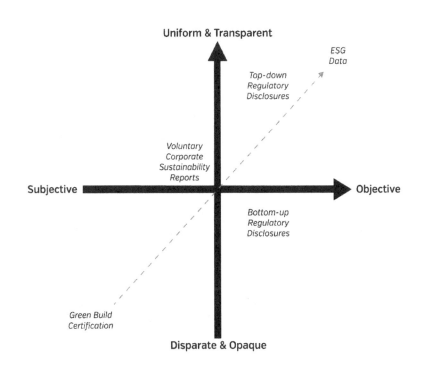

Green building certifications are not only disparate (there are many of them) and opaque (building assessments are not publicly available) in nature, but they are also subjective, since each certification has its own criteria. They are therefore not a source of actionable information. Voluntary corporate sustainability reports are also largely subjective, since companies draft them based on their own chosen set of criteria and emphasize the points they wish to make to their stakeholders. Voluntary sustainability reports are more transparent than Green building certifications simply because they are made public to the market. Yet their uniformity is arguable, since there is no standard structure used for all reports. Even within specific industry sectors, the presentation and data provided in these reports can differ significantly, depending on the narrative the company wishes to tell.

Pure ESG data, on the other hand, is entirely uniform, transparent, and objective, and is therefore the most actionable form of information available to the marketplace. The limitations of ESG data are only as far as its adoption in the marketplace.

The information derived from regulatory disclosures is comparably more objective than the information that can be derived from Green building certifications and voluntary corporate sustainability reports— especially if there is a proscribed framework for the disclosures. For one thing, top-down regulation usually aims to proscribe thresholds for national targets and to punish noncompliant market participants. Green certification programs, on the other hand, do not punish bad actors. They simply award the so-called best-in-class. Another key difference is that regulators need to be transparent in the frameworks they create, since laws are a matter of public record and need to hold up to scrutiny—and transparency breeds rigor in the face of the market's critique.

Now, admittedly, there are two assumptions in the assertion that regulatory disclosures are more objective than the information derived from voluntary frameworks. The first and most obvious assumption is that the government establishing the rules does so under the basic tenets of the Rule of Law—i.e., the rules are clear, stable, publicized, and fair.[13] The second assumption is that the rules are developed using scientific methods for identifying the harm they wish to prohibit and the benchmarks they wish to set (for instance, carbon emissions levels). Yet, as long as these assumptions are met, the information derived from a regulatory framework is much more objective, transparent— and actionable—than corporate sustainability reports as they are currently used. The information is also far more objective than that which can be derived from a Green certification.

Top-down frameworks provide the most uniform information since companies under the one regime must adhere to the same structure of disclosure. Individual bottom-up frameworks may well have reporting proscriptions that result in transparent disclosures, but their patchwork nature—the fact that there might be many different regulators at the local, state, or national level, or because the regulator allows companies to choose their own framework—ultimately inject opacity into the mix.

When it comes to the compliance of sustainability frameworks within the construction industry, transparency, uniformity, and objectivity is highly valued. A developer would prefer to have consistent yardsticks, rather than having to negotiate disparate rules and regulations depending on whether they are in New York, Chicago, L.A., or Albuquerque. They would rather spend their time and money ensuring adherence to regulations, rather than on obtaining a Green certification plaque to put on their wall.

Regulation is the great equalizer. It is not pay-to-play, like a certification. When drafted correctly, regulation takes into consideration all of society's stakeholders—citizens, businesses, government, and the planet—rather than merely what might be an adequate level of sustainability to market to consumers.

As the market moves from voluntary certification to regulatory compliance of sustainability, it is acknowledging the materiality of ESG factors and the necessity of using objective measures.

Returning to the example of the Pure Food Act of 1906, it seems that it is only by developing strict and enforceable regulation of sustainability that we will be able to move sustainability from something that is considered abstract to the core DNA of the capitalist system.

Enforcement is key

As well as objectivity, uniformity, and transparency, to ensure that market participants do the right thing a sustainability framework needs enforceability. In a regime that is regulated by the government, bad actors can be sanctioned for noncompliance. Their businesses can be shut down. But these mechanisms do not exist in a voluntary regime. Sanctions are not part of the Green building certification model. Show me a time LEED ever took away a certification for any other reason than the certified company was unable to pay LEED's fee.

The enforceability of voluntary frameworks versus regulation

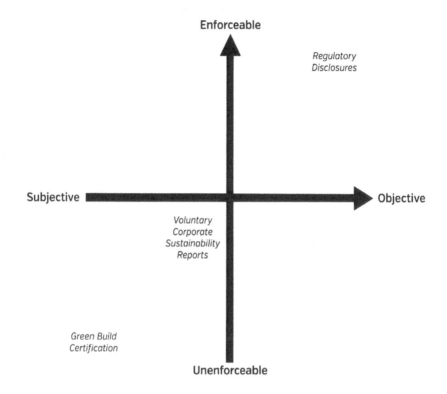

Although it carries a big stick, sustainability regulation is not the bogeyman, and it is not unwelcomed for most market participants. It is my view that we should celebrate the fact that as a society we are heading towards regulating adherence to sustainability standards. The carrot has not brought us to where we need to be. It is time for the stick. Better rules mean better outcomes for everyone.

Let us not forget that there is a need for accurate, transparent, and objective information on sustainability, based on ESG metrics. Punishing bad actors is an important part of maintaining the flow of that information. But it will not come from a voluntary framework that has only reached 5% market penetration and is designed to reward gold stars to people who pay enough money for them.

In fact, it is my belief that the rise of regulatory frameworks for sustainability will ultimately lead to the demise of Green building certifications as we know them today. Both cannot operate in the same space. If regulations require one set of compliance criteria and Green certifications another, one will ultimately lose.

How ratings are moving the needle

Parallel to the rise of regulation based on ESG criteria is another trend that is moving the market towards greater transparency of sustainability information: The move towards rating systems for green bonds.

As discussed in the previous chapter, a bond rating is a transparent statement about the risk exposure of a credit instrument such as sovereign debt or a corporate bond. A bond rating quantifies the quality and creditworthiness of bonds and bond issuers so that market participants can objectively decide what bonds they wish to invest in, given their appetite for risk. Traditional bonds are evaluated by looking at a company's financial information, including balance sheet, competition, macroeconomic factors, and the issuer's profit outlook.

Green bonds are credit instruments that add another layer of criteria on top of the traditional financial metrics—specifically that the funds raised be earmarked for climate or environmental projects. The first green bond was issued in 2007[14] and since then the market has grown to $1 trillion market capitalization.[15] While this is only a fraction of the estimated $120 trillion global bond market, it nonetheless represents significant growth from $11 billion in 2011.

A recent study of the green bond market in Sweden—which is both one of the more mature markets and is also representative of European and American green bond trends—found that the advent of green bonds has led to more investors using the capital markets to engage on environmental issues.[16] green bonds have established a "new infrastructure," according to the study, consisting of:

- Guidelines for what counts as a Green investment
- The development of corporate frameworks that provide transparency on how proceeds will be used
- External validation of the credibility of issuers' green bond frameworks
- A system for companies to report to investors on the use of proceeds and their environmental impacts

Green bonds are an incredibly useful innovation for channeling capital into projects earmarked for environmental and sustainable projects, and their growth is expected to continue. But there is another logical step that bond ratings will likely follow in the not-too-distant future: The application of ESG criteria to all bonds—not just green bonds. The logic is simple: If ESG metrics are material to the risk profile of an investment, then they are material to a business's ability to perform. Therefore, they are material to a business's ability to repay debt. Taken to its logical conclusion, every bond should (to some degree) take ESG metrics into consideration.

Yet green bonds as they exist today are by no means perfect. Currently, there are certain issues with green bonds that need to be addressed. The Swedish study found that while investors frequently believed that their purchase of a green bond meant that their money was financing a new and novel project to combat climate change or improve the environment, often these bonds were financing pre-existing environmental projects.

However, as the market matures and regulatory frameworks take national carbon emission goals into consideration, it is distinctly possible that the regulation of green bonds will include provisions aimed at (1) ensuring that funds are used for new projects rather than pre-existing projects, and/or (2) bond issuers must be transparent about such arrangements. If an issuer is making explicit claims about their sustainability outcomes, and their bond is based on the idea that it is contributing to the health of the environment, then it is obvious that the market will inevitably demand transparency over such claims.

And green bonds are just the tip of the iceberg. New bond innovations are now a regular occurrence in the marketplace, with blue bonds aimed at marine conservation activities, brown bonds created to help shift high carbon-dependent companies Green, and gender bonds to improve gender equality. Yet as creative as these new forms of financing may be, they are all but gimmickry if their goals are not independently audited and their performance measured by standardized metrics. Because, in the end, purpose-build bonds are not just about raising capital, they should also be delivering impact.

Green bond ratings and sustainability regulation are also seeing a convergence. In July 2021, the EU launched a green bond framework to help Europe meet its climate goals. The European Green Bond Standard aimed to drive money into projects that helped the continent meet its climate goal of net zero carbon emissions by the middle of this century. Unlike other bond standards, the EU's standard is based on a taxonomy developed by the EU and only allows activities that it considers to be Green.

The proceeds of a European Green Bond must be invested in projects aimed to fulfill one of the five environmental objectives outlined in the taxonomy:

1. Climate change mitigation

4. Biodiversity conservation

2. Climate change adaptation

5. Pollution prevention and control

3. Natural resource conservation

The EU plans to provide more rigorous oversight of companies that choose to follow its standard. It expects full transparency and detailed reporting on how the bond proceeds are allocated. It will require an external review to ensure compliance with EU regulations and taxonomy alignment of the funded projects. Reviewers will be supervised by the EU's financial watchdog, the European Securities Markets Authority (ESMA).

Yet many investment experts believe stricter oversight will not deter bond issuers from using it. In fact, many believe the more rigorous oversight will drive greater adoption, since transparency and rigor are what investors have been calling for. Issuers that fall foul of the EU's disclosure rules can be fined by their national financial regulator.[17]

When it comes to broadening the market's understanding and acceptance of sustainability and ESG metrics, regulation will be an enablement function. When governments regulate an industry, it becomes mainstream, accepted, and normalized. Consider the cannabis industry in the United States, which trades publicly and legally in a substance that only a decade ago was nationally prohibited.

By some estimates, the legal cannabis market in the United States in 2020 was worth around $17 billion—up 46% year-over-year. By 2021, some 14 states have already permitted adults to use cannabis products for recreational purposes, while 36 allowed medical sales of the drug.[18] A large contributor to that growth, say industry analysts, is the enforcement of Cannabis regulations—which many believe is a sign of a maturing market. The enacting of Cannabis market regulation literally enabled the creation of a multibillion-dollar market.

Regulation is an enablement function. And the rating, the credit markets, and the capital markets are the fulfillment.

Chapter 5:
ESG is Changing What is Material to Society and the Markets

The market's increasing desire for accurate and measurable data on a building's performance should not come as a surprise. The capital and real estate markets are a product of human behavior, and it is human nature to want to understand such a phenomenon by quantifying it. When we ascertain how to measure something, we set about counting it as precisely as we can.

Take nutrition and diet, for example. We understand that certain foods are healthy for us and that we should eat a balanced diet composed of foods from each of the major food groups—fruit and vegetables, protein, grains, and dairy. However, more than simply understanding the main food groups, we have also come to understand what consuming specific types and quantities of foods and substances do to the human body. Equipped with this ability to measure the scientific qualities of the food we eat, humans will measure grams of fat, carbohydrates, salt, and any other qualities that we know can impact our health.

These measures need to be accurate, or we do not find them useful. If a person is attempting to gain or lose weight, they desire to know specifically how many calories are contained in a specific food product. If they are serious about their quest to add or gain weight, they are not satisfied with simply knowing a basic range. It is not enough to say that a burger or chocolate bar has between 100 and 2,000 calories. People watching their weight want to precisely know the calories of their food, so that they can control their caloric input.

Some dieters want to know exactly how much fat or carbohydrates are in the food products they consume, so that they can make an informed decision about their energy intake. Diabetics generally need to avoid foods high in sugar, while people with high blood pressure need to watch the quantity of salt they consume. People with certain allergies—such as legumes, gluten, dairy, or shellfish—must ensure the foods they ingest are free from allergens which affect them and can make them ill.

The myriad reasons why individual humans—and humanity as a whole—desire to watch what they eat in terms of both calories and the nutritional value of what we consume—has led to detailed food and nutrition labeling rules and regulations.

While it is true that people might not regularly read these food labels, or pay too much attention to their detail, such labeling—and the accuracy of the measurement behind them—is vitally important to a large proportion of the population for a vast array of reasons. Without reading these labels and being able to rely on the accuracy of the information they contain, some people might simply put on a few more pounds than they would otherwise prefer. Others would literally die.

Ultimately, the point of food labels is to accurately inform those who require accurate information. You might not need this information all the time, but when you do, you need to be able to trust that the data is correct.

Even if a person decides not to carefully read the nutrition labels of the food they consume, they are nonetheless likely aware of the science behind them. They are also likely to understand the basic principles of healthy eating—such as knowing that an excess of sugar or salt is not good for you. This understanding of basic nutrition is a product of centuries of research and is based on a foundation of science that provides a high degree of confidence.

Multiple studies have found that food nutrition labeling—whether on products in supermarkets[1] or on menu items in chain restaurants[2]—has positively modified consumer behavior when it comes to selecting healthier food options. The very fact of being able to measure and communicate this necessary nutritional data leads to positive behavior.

Yet the power of food labels—and the communication of the data they contain—is also a product of their ubiquity. It is important that this data can be trusted—that it is based on science. But I do not believe nutritional labels would work as effectively in modifying behavior if they were not so omnipresent and easy to understand. Because we see them on every product that we pick up in the supermarket, we take notice of them. Their usefulness comes from the fact that they are everywhere, and they can be trusted.

The closest example to nutritional labels in the ESG world is the ENERGY STAR ratings system. This measure, prominently displayed on white goods and household electrical appliances in every electronics store, has also been shown to improve consumer behavior when it comes to selecting household electrical appliances.[3] Because if they are easy to find and prominently displayed at time of purchase, consumers—albeit sometimes subconsciously—will take notice of these labels and incorporate the data into their purchasing behavior.

The automotive industry also provides salient examples of how universally understood metrics for measurement improve our understanding of a product, inform consumer choice, and help regulate the utility of an asset.

When consumers purchase used motor vehicles, whatever the type of vehicle—motorcycle, sedan, SUV, gasoline, diesel, electric, or hybrid—there is a well-established set of criteria that most buyers will follow. These criteria are heavily dependent on widely recognized benchmarks of standardized and accurate data.

After selecting make, model, and year of manufacture, most purchasers want to know mileage and fuel consumption. These two figures provide purchasers with key information about a used car's life expectancy and its efficiency.

The number of miles or kilometers on a car's odometer shows how much distance a car has traveled over the course of its life. This measure is a useful indication of the wear and tear that a vehicle has sustained over time. A car with higher mileage is likely to be costlier to maintain than a car with fewer miles on the odometer.

Approximations of mileage are not enough for most vehicle buyers. A used car salesperson will not close many sales by telling a prospect that a car's mileage is between 100 and 100,000 miles. Most mechanics believe that an average of around 12,000 miles a year shows that a car has not been overdriven. They may also recommend that a car with more than 100,000 miles on the odometer is at higher risk of needing frequent repairs and has a shorter potential engine life (many modern cars are thought to have a maximum life of around 150,000 miles). For this reason, buyers want an accurate odometer reading before they make a vehicle purchase.

Neither will simply guessing a car's fuel consumption satisfy a discerning vehicle purchaser. They will want to know precisely how efficient their prospective new car is.

Fuel consumption data measures the distance a vehicle can travel based on the amount of fuel it requires to travel that distance. Whether it be miles per gallon, kilometers per liter, or (for electric vehicles) miles per gallon equivalent, responsible buyers always take fuel efficiency into consideration. These buyers require accurate statistics based on uniform measures, both for highway and city driving.

Larger vehicles such as SUVs will have less fuel efficiency than economy hatchbacks, but an MPG measure is equally useful to benchmark classes of vehicle against each other.

The data derived from Green certification does not resemble the data that dieters obtain from calorie counts and nutrition labels, nor the data that vehicle purchasers obtain from odometer readings and fuel consumption statistics.

As we have seen in previous chapters, Green certifications cannot provide the function of actionable data for investors in the built environment. The various types of certifications—BREEAM, LEED, etc.—are not comparable to each other; they do not provide the same data that can be compared to each other. Even as a collective, certifications are not ubiquitous; they cannot provide a benchmark of every building on the planet. Every car on the planet has an odometer.

Every packaged food product in a supermarket has a nutrition label. Not every product on the planet has a Green certification.

Consider once more our intrepid real estate investor. Faced with the choice of three otherwise identical buildings—one BREEAM certified, one LEED certified, and one not certified at all—she cannot derive much in the way of conclusions about the sustainability of the three investment opportunities. One could argue that the non-certified building might be the least sustainable. However, this assumption can easily be proven wrong.

A lack of certification does not *per se* imply that the building is not Green or energy efficient. It simply means that the building has not been certified by one of the Green certification providers. There may be plenty of reasons why the building developers and operators chose not to pursue certification. They may have felt certification was too costly, or they might have preferred to use their capital instead to conduct tangible improvements to the building. The developers and operators might have their own new and innovative model of what constitutes a Green building, and current Green building certifications might be slow to catch up with their innovations.

Whatever the reason, the non-certified building could very well be the most sustainable, yet without uniform data and measurements there would be no way to know.

It is worth remembering that the overall building stock of certified buildings is but a small percentage (just over 1%) of the entire built universe in the United States. Yet these other 99% of buildings exist. They are real bricks-and-mortar, and they represent the vast majority of the built environment. Buildings that are not certified still have a carbon footprint; it simply hasn't been evaluated by a certification program.

Remember the igloo from Chapter 3? An igloo consumes no energy. It is resource efficient, and its building materials are entirely natural and produced by hand. In its environment, the igloo is purpose-built and resilient, and it would be difficult to imagine a more environmentally perfect and sustainable structure. But there is not an igloo on the planet that has been Green certified. Many building owners and operators in cities and towns across the planet are striving to become as energy efficient as possible—either for a desire to be better stewards of their environment or for purely economic motives.

These building operators may be using LED lights in every fitting, conserving their water usage, and limiting their waste, but they choose not to pursue Green certification. Just because a building is not certified, does not mean it is not Green. Similarly, just because a building is certified does not mean it is Green by all definitions and measures. Furthermore, I would argue that in fact there is no such thing as a Green building or a non-Green building. There are just buildings, which exist on a spectrum, from the most energy efficient and sustainable, to the most inefficient with outsized carbon footprints.

Each building has the intrinsic qualities of a building—materials, energy usage, carbon footprint—and each has the potential to improve their sustainability. These buildings simply need the metrics to help them accomplish this transition. In fact, I would argue that by concentrating on the so-called best performers, Green certifications divert our attention away from the buildings that truly matter in the fight against climate change: underperforming buildings. It is the buildings that are net polluters, the energy inefficient buildings, and the buildings with outsized carbon footprints that we should really be concentrating on and helping to improve.

To my mind—and I think the minds of most investors—the construction sector and real estate industry's time, energy, and capital is not well spent chasing the approval of one of the various Green certification providers or following their proprietary certification methodology. Instead, the best outcome for the world—and for the marketplace—is ubiquitous data on all the various environmental, social, and governance factors that provide a holistic view of a building's physical state, its impact on people and the planet, its management, and its risk exposure. In short, a building's sustainability as a physical asset and its viability as an investment.

Green building certifications are not standardized and ubiquitous. Certifications cannot provide the equivalent of a building's calorie count, mileage, or odometer reading. But ESG data could. ESG metrics as a standard across the entire built environment would go a long way to helping more buildings improve.

Measuring what's material

As we have seen in previous chapters, investors want granular information on a number of measurable factors. In the environmental realm, such factors include carbon footprint and waste output, energy usage, and water consumption. Investors want this information not only historically, but as a projection for future performance, including what owners are doing to improve those numbers over time.

One of the principal drivers behind the desire for environmental data is a growing understanding of physical climate risk. Every real estate asset on the planet is subject to one or more types of climate hazards, whether it be threats posed by extreme heat or cold, hurricanes, wildfires, or flooding. Buildings cannot simply be picked up and moved, so investors want to know how aware owners are of the risks their assets face, and what real estate operators are doing to mitigate those risks.

Society is also becoming increasingly aware of the risk on real estate assets posed by inattention to social and governance factors. In the real estate sector, social and governance considerations now extend far beyond whether a company has fair hiring practices, diverse leadership, and a culture of inclusion. Such requirements have become base level, and can more easily be measured quantifiably, for instance by examining the demographics of employees and board members.

Real estate investors now want more precise data on how a building performs based on a wider list of measures of impact. Real estate has the power to foster community engagement, for instance, by being more aware of the community's cultural needs and by listening to community members during the design and building phase. Real estate operators can provide more affordable access to better amenities and public spaces for lower income neighborhoods.

Sustainable building management can reduce harmful environmental effects on neighboring communities by improving their waste and water usage. Landlords can build a healthier environment for their tenants by improving interior air quality and making better use of shared spaces. Investors, desiring more exact data on these factors, will no longer take a building operator's word that such activities are taking place. Instead, efforts and policies need to be measured, benchmarked, and documented.

As the real estate industry moves through the maturity curve from vague notions of Green to measurable ESG metrics, factors such as environmental, social, and governance considerations need to become more evidence based. In the same way that the investors who drive real estate markets use financial data, they now use ESG data.

In the same way that consumers make dietary decisions based on nutrition labels and car purchases based on mileage and MPG, investors make real estate decisions based on an expanded set of criteria that now includes measures of sustainability.

The Era of Green was aspirational and characterized with a lofty idea of doing good. However, it contained limited actionable data. The market's migration toward ESG is characterized by data-driven, objective, and measurable goals. The market is moving towards consensus over what is material—in other words, what information is important and relevant. In real estate, like the broader market, it is coalescing around ESG.

We have known for decades that certain factors are material to our understanding of the operations and value of a building. Energy and electrons cost money; building operators buy them from a utility company and that cost impacts a building's operating costs. Investors consider the cost of energy material, and building operators attempt to reduce that cost as best they can.

Subsequently, it turns out that energy usage is also a material contributor to carbon emissions. As such, it was relatively easy for the market to evolve from an understanding that energy is material, to realizing that carbon emissions were also material. Energy efficiency and carbon emissions are two sides of the same coin.

Yet in my experience, it has taken a long time for the real estate market to move beyond an understanding of the materiality of carbon emissions to the materiality of other ESG factors. For decades, energy efficiency has almost been an analogue for sustainability. I believe there are two reasons for this industry's focus on energy efficiency. The first is because of the obvious importance of decreasing our carbon footprint and becoming more energy efficient. However, the second reason for this preoccupation with energy—I believe—is because energy cost is the most easily measurable of a building's environmental factors.

Energy consumption is measurable, and what is measurable is material.

What I mean by this is that it is only when we can truly measure an object or concept that we find it material.

The earth's ozone layer is a poignant and historic example. As early as 1912, explorers in the Antarctic noticed unusual clouds over the polar stratosphere. These were believed to be ozone—a gas discovered in the Nineteenth Century, around the same time that it was discovered that harmful ultraviolet rays from the sun were absorbed in the earth's stratosphere. Yet it was not until the 1950s that British scientists set up an observatory that was able to measure ozone using a Dobson Spectrophotometer. Without the ability to measure ozone depletion and the link to increased radiation coming from the sun, the impact of CFCs (chlorofluorocarbons) would not have been understood to be material.[4]

Things we think are material are the things that we can measure.
And if we cannot measure them, we assume that they must not be
material.

In the investment world, financial data has never really suffered this problem in the same way that ESG data has. Profits and losses are material. Liabilities and debts are material. It is relatively easy—when there is full disclosure of a company's financial information—to understand the value of a company based on its financial data, which is why the traditional way to measure a company's value was financial measurement. Financial data has always been considered material.

One of the challenges of the ESG framework is moving the needle on what is material and what constitutes a measurable factor. In a way, ESG has fallen into the same trap I described above: Only things which we can measure are presumed to be material.

What do I mean by this? While ESG has become increasingly important to investors and society as a whole, we seem to only be focusing on a small number of factors that we can easily measure and are financial in nature. And this has been to the neglect of the full range of important—and material—ESG factors.

By financial in nature, I mean ESG factors that are easily representable in a company's financial results or can be easily quantified by attributing a price to them. For instance, it is easy to price energy, but how do you put a price on human health or a building's impact on its local community?

Human health and impact on community are material, yet their measurability presents genuine challenges that proponents of ESG must face. Otherwise, such factors will continue to lack the perception of materiality.

All is not lost, however. The market is beginning to understand how to quantify hitherto unmeasurable material ESG factors.

Health and wellbeing become material

Even before the global coronavirus pandemic and its resultant quarantines and lockdowns, most humans spent around 90% of their time indoors. As such, our health has always been substantially influenced by the buildings that we occupy and spend our time in—our homes, schools, and workplaces.

Yet it is incredibly difficult to measure a building's impact on human health. How does a person's physical space impact their cardiac or mental health? What would such a measure look like? I am certainly unaware of any economic measure—at least not one that can scale to a universal benchmark for the real estate industry. When we do not have an economic measure, it is very difficult to obtain the materiality of a variable or factor like health and wellbeing.

However, recently there has been some progress in certain areas of the health and wellbeing components of ESG—specifically around air quality.

As a reaction to the recent pandemic, and as managers began planning the return to office for their workforces, the subject of air quality in the workplace took center stage. The pandemic, said experts, presented a "once-in-a-generation" opportunity to make workers healthier and happier by improving indoor air quality.[5]

At the time, there was a growing movement to insist that organizations—and by extension, building operators—measure and monitor the air quality of workplaces.

What has yet to be seen, however, is how the market will price air quality as an ESG metric, and whether the market will consider it material in a company's performance. Will the market punish organizations that do not provide good air quality to their workforce? Will it reward organizations that do provide positive indoor air quality?

Whether or not the market directly prices such information would be the most obvious and direct use of air quality becoming material. There are other ways. For instance, air quality could be used to understand the potential productivity of a company's workforce (more on this shortly).

Ultimately, the challenge for ESG is to move the market past its preoccupation with measures that look and feel like financial measures (profit and loss, debt, and the monetary prices of material factors such as energy), and obtain an agreement that there are nonetheless measures that are not economic—for instance, human health and wellbeing—that are also material.

Put another way, the market needs a way to recognize factors that are material that may not be economic. We need to get past the dollars-and-cents per square foot of energy consumption and enter the dollars-and-cents per square foot equivalent of the human benefit of healthier environments.

These factors could be issues such as the benefit of providing the ideal study environment, or the benefit of an environment that is comfortable and conducive to productive work. We generally understand the benefits of office spaces that are fit for purpose—no one wants to work in an office that is dirty or stuffy. However, taking an ESG metric approach would require us to be able to measure and benchmark factors such as comfortability, and the health and wellbeing of workers using a particular space.

Experimenting with new measures

One possible measure could be the productivity of labor per square foot of office space. Since the largest single cost in a business is typically its people, followed closely by its real estate, any dollar spent on real estate that can provide a marginal improvement in the productivity of an organization's labor force becomes extremely valuable.

In 2016, Jones Lang LaSalle published a study postulating what it termed the "3-30-300" rule. The theory maintains that, per square foot, the average order of magnitude between an organization's utilities, rent, and payroll costs is:

$3 for utilities,

$30 for rent, and

$300 for payroll.

For instance, if a real estate operating company spends $30 million on payroll, it will likely spend around $300,000 on rent and $30,000 on utilities.

JLL recognized that actual figures fluctuate from location to location, and organization to organization. However, the company maintained that 3-30-300 was a useful rule of thumb.

Using the 3-30-300 rule, says JLL, companies can understand the true operating costs of a building, and that contrary to popular belief, rent and utility costs are not the source of primary gains. For instance, using the 3-30-300 rule, JLL posits that increasing energy efficiency by 10% saves around 30 cents per square foot and decreasing rent by 10% generates $3/square foot in savings. Yet a 10% boost in staff productivity yields $30 per square foot in benefits.

JLL's assertion is that building operators can improve their energy efficiency and enjoy cost savings, but they can also dramatically improve their value by implementing environmental modifications that improve employee productivity, such as indoor acoustics, air quality, humidity, lighting, and temperature.

One of the most interesting aspects of the JLL study is that it attempts to quantify common sense ideas. We intuitively understand that if workers inhabit a healthier and more comfortable environment, it stands to reason that they will be more productive—for instance, they can better concentrate on their work instead of being distracted by the office temperature, they will remain healthier and take fewer sick days, and in a well-lit environment they see their work more clearly and make less errors. In fact, recent studies have found air quality and natural light have the biggest impact on employee wellbeing.

Admittedly, tying these concepts to economic measures has proved difficult and has been disputed. Yet it is worth observing that the challenge of ESG is to begin establishing genuine financial measures such as these, and therefore make material of what we all understand intuitively should be material—our wellbeing and our performance at work. I have been surprised that the market has been so slow to grasp these ideas.

Quantifying the seemingly qualitative

As long as we are impacted by climate change, the mainstays of measuring sustainability will continue to be energy efficiency, carbon footprint and, increasingly, water usage.

As a society and as a market, we have struggled with human health and wellbeing, even though in recent years we have grown more aware of the impact of factors such as indoor air quality on health. We have struggled with understanding the value of indirect benefits such as a building development's benefits to the community, even as we increase, for instance, our understanding of the impact of unequal access to housing.

Aesthetics have also proved difficult to quantify—especially in terms of a building design's effect on the community in which it is located. While we are all aware that attractive architecture is generally more desirable than ugly buildings, it is still incredibly difficult to surmise and quantify the benefits to the community of investing in high design and other aesthetic elements.

When the layperson identifies a new building that they like, it is to the building's architectural design that they will usually first be drawn—a modern flair, an inspiring profile, impressive height, or innovative and attractive use of open spaces. Invariably these new buildings will be Green buildings, and a discussion of the building's sustainability will soon follow the discussion of the building's aesthetics.

Increasingly, the casual observer's conversation will turn to a building's impact on the local community, yet we as a society struggle to articulate—let alone quantify and evaluate—such fuzzy concepts. Society and the markets need to ascertain how to measure these aspects of a building's ESG profile. Because until they are measured, they will not be managed, and they will not be considered material.

Real estate owners and investors rarely cared about the health of a building, or a building's impact on its occupants' health until recently. Beginning in the last 30 years of the 20th Century, several cities around the world experienced incidents of their buildings literally making people sick. Legionnaires Disease in the 1970s, Sick Building Syndrome beginning in the 1980s, SARS (severe acute respiratory syndrome) first identified in the 2000s, and now COVID-19, have made us fundamentally rethink the impact of the built environment on our health. Now, building owners and investors realize they need to care not only about the impact of climate on the built environment and the built environment's impact on climate, but also the built environment's impact on human health and wellbeing.

No smoke means no fire?

Society has drawn a hard line at some of the visceral threats that buildings can impose—such as catching fire from faulty wiring and exploding from ruptured gas mains. We try to protect building tenants from these risks by regulating against such threats and sanctioning bad actors whose action (or inaction) leads to loss of life. However, what if the danger is not something that is as immediate as a fire or explosion?

When threats are harder to identify or cause harm over long periods of time, they are more difficult to understand and to regulate.

Consider the health threats caused by asbestos. People have been using asbestos to make pots and insulate buildings since 2,400 BC, and in the first century AD, Roman scholars documented incidents of asbestos mine slaves becoming ill. Yet in the 1850s, during the industrial revolution, asbestos became a key building component. In 1918 the U.S. government recognized that asbestos workers died earlier than the average worker and in the 1930s that there was a link between asbestos exposure and cancer, yet it was not until 1967 and 1971 (in the UK, and U.S. respectively) that the first successful personal injury cases against asbestos and employer negligence were won.[6] The journey from our understanding of its danger to our eventual regulation of its use was a slow road.

When society can't see the smoke, it is reticent to yell "fire." Even when it does understand the risk associated with a certain activity, there can still be a significant lag between identification of the threat and society's response—whether it be via legislative or judicial action. In the same way as it took decades for modern society to respond to the threat posed by asbestos, society and lawmakers have struggled with the issue of climate change.

The science around the impact of human-made climate change has been around for decades, yet we have been slow to act. When it comes to large, existential threats, society seems to persist in a state of collective cognitive dissonance. Unless the phenomena can be measured.

If you sat people down in the early Twentieth Century and explained the risk asbestos posed to building inhabitants, I am sure they would have understood and agreed that something should be done about it. But it took decades—ostensibly until building owners were losing their livelihoods through litigation—that anything was done. I would argue that it was not until the threat of asbestos exposure could be quantified in potential dollars lost to litigation, that there was any movement in the market to change corporate behaviors.

While we have understood the risk posed by Legionnaires' disease, sick building syndrome, and SARS for decades, I believe it was not until the Coronavirus pandemic that indoor air quality truly began to become a primary concern to tenants and the occupiers of offices, schools, factories, and other workplaces.

By early 2021, demand for air quality monitors began booming, with market analysts predicting exponential growth for years to come.[7] Now, air quality is material. And it is possible that this new focus on air quality may be what breaks the dam on a flood of new ESG data factors for the built environment.

Unlike many of the ESG factors that have come before—including energy efficiency and carbon footprints—air quality opens up a conversation about the link between a building's condition and the health and wellbeing of its occupiers. The conversation about air quality is one of health and safety—at its extreme it is the statement: If the air quality is dangerous, it will kill me.

However, the subject of air quality quickly leads into wellbeing subjects such as comfortability, and suddenly the conversation turns economic. As a tenant or investor, I expect building operators to provide a safe environment. But I also expect a comfortable environment—otherwise I will not sign a lease or invest in the property.

A 2015 study drew a direct line between air quality and worker productivity. The researchers found that just a small change in ventilation could increase the performance of workers by 8%—an improvement equivalent to a $6500 increase in employee annual productivity—and reduced absenteeism.[8]

New research has also linked indoor air quality to improved performance of students. One recent study found that exposing students to poor indoor air quality during the school term preceding a test led to significant decreases in performance. The study found that one standard deviation increase in average CO2 during the school term led to a 0.14 standard deviation drop in test scores.[9]

Once its economic factors can be measured, air quality becomes material.

Inequality becomes measurable

Health and wellbeing are not the only social ESG criteria that will increasingly become measurable and material. Chief among the other ESG factors that are becoming important to both society as a whole and real estate investors specifically, is diversity and equality.

Of course, the importance of diversity and equality is not at all new—the lack of these has been a blight on society for centuries. Apart from the obvious fairness and justice of equality, a society where all people have an equal chance to participate in the economy as productive members of society is so obviously advantageous to all members of society and the markets. As we saw in previous chapters, diversity and inclusion has already become an important part of corporate social responsibility and is a major platform of good governance generally.

On a corporate level, diversity can be measured in terms of the diversity of a workforce or a supplier base, and activist investors are increasingly pressuring boards to become more diverse. However, my prediction for the future is that diversity and inclusion will also become a specific, measurable, and material factor for real estate investors.

Real estate will become one of the future battlegrounds for race equality, not because it is just and proper that everyone has equal access to real estate—although they certainly should—but because diversity and inclusion are material to real estate investment returns. Why? The argument is similar to the health and wellbeing aspects of real estate. A healthy and safe building that promotes its occupant's wellbeing is a more reliable and less risky investment than one which does not.

In the same way, I am certain that in time, the diversity of tenants and building occupiers, and the equality and inclusiveness of a real estate investment's operations and management, will be proven to be a key and measurable factor for its viability and performance as an investment. Better buildings have more diversity, and buildings that attract a diverse clientele are considered healthy and for the benefit of all tenants in a building. Countless studies on the benefits of diversity in building tenants—and the dangers of segregation—have shown that diverse residential buildings and communities elevate both the economic and social wellbeing of the community as a whole.[10]

For instance, I believe we will see the conversation around what is truly material in a real estate investment move toward the affordability of multifamily residences, the diversity of the occupants within the building, and other such diversity and inclusion factors.

Diversity in real estate is already starting to be measured to a certain degree. In some markets, real estate developers are either required or encouraged to set aside a portion of their development for affordable housing, which can go some way toward improving real estate ownership rates in minority communities. Governments may define specific criteria, such as setting the rent that a building operator can charge for the affordable housing component of their development. In other jurisdictions, governments might provide building developers with tax breaks for providing affordable housing.

Even in residential real estate, such as private multifamily housing, I have started to see affordability begin to become a factor to investors. Investors are beginning to ask whether developments will be attractive and affordable to a broader range of purchasers and tenants beyond middle class white people, so that they can understand if a development or neighborhood will be diverse.

Investors are beginning to tell real estate developers that they believe a development will be more durable and more sustainable if it targets a better income-to-rent ratio and a broader cross section of the market, rather than simply trying to maximize rental income for the property.

The rationale is that if a greater number of people do not have to spend a large proportion of their income on rent (and therefore have a much larger disposable income for bills, family, and life in general), they will be happier tenants and more likely to stay for a longer period of time. Long-term tenants mean less turnover and a more reliable income stream for investors.

The opportunity to do good

In 2017, the U.S. federal government created a new investment designation which provided tax benefits for investments in lower income areas. So-called Opportunity Zone Funds are designed to encourage investors to put their capital to work in ways that benefit impoverished communities around the United States. Investors receive tax breaks if they invest in new businesses in these Opportunity Zones over a number of years.[11] The hope is that sustained investment will provide a source of jobs and economic growth for low-income communities.

While the government does not directly use sustainability or ESG criteria in their assessment of an investment, many high net worth and institutional investors approach Opportunity Funds as an ESG opportunity, since their investment goals are more than simply monetary—ostensibly they are trying to improve a community.[12]

More broadly, opportunity zones are part of the wider trend of regulation or policy considering how investments can help society. By providing tax benefits and defining a framework for how an investor's capital must be spent to the betterment of society, Opportunity Zone Funds are an example of measuring an investment's success based on more than simply its monetary gains. Philosophically, I believe Opportunity Zone Funds are also an acknowledgement that there are other gains which we seek in a real estate investment beyond profits.

Solar power purchase agreements (PPAs) are another example of investments that provide financial returns but also claim to help solve an ESG problem. Solar PPAs are financial agreements where a third-party developer finances and installs solar panels on someone else's property. The property owner receives stable, low-cost electricity, while the solar services provider receives the income generated from the sale of the electricity generated by the solar panels.

Opportunity zones and solar PPAs are just two of the many examples of investments that seek outcomes other than simply financial. I believe that over time, the market will see even more of these examples, and the measures of choice for such funds will be ESG metrics. ESG has the potential to help all stakeholders—investors, regulators, asset operators, and the public at large—understand what is material.

For now, we face a fascinating yet dire conundrum: How do we measure what is material, and how do we make what is material measurable? One of the core arguments of this book is that markets can work, but markets without perfect information cannot work perfectly. The notable consequence of imperfect markets is climate catastrophe and social inequity.

When it comes to what is material to society, the markets have not done the best job they could. Centuries of a blinkered focus on quarterly profits and growth for growth's sake has brought us to a point that is unsustainable. But that is not to say that capitalism is the root of all evil. Quite the opposite.

The capital markets, in tandem with a robust regulatory framework, have the potential to right the ship on climate change and income equality. Market dynamics have the potential to refocus our attention on solving the problems we face today. However, to do this, the markets themselves need to be refocused. No longer can exponential growth be the goal at the expense of all other factors.

Over the past few years, market consensus has begun to change. Market participants are hungry for more—perfect—information on the measures that are material to success. ESG is the framework that will deliver this perfect information to a more perfect market. The market is heading in this direction. The question is: can it get there fast enough to make a difference?

Conclusion:
Building Better

Readers of this book will have already guessed by now that 'Green' is not exactly my favorite word. Green is a color. It is a convenient and widely recognized term connoting all manner of environmentally responsible activities. It does little, however, to describe the actual performance, or lack thereof, of buildings, real estate portfolios, lenders, or insurers. To do that, we must look at the data. The term 'sustainability' suffers from similar limitations.

As a concept, it's directionally correct. As a business term, we must be more specific.

Just like the word 'Green,' sustainability is much too broad and overused as a tool for marketers and corporate communications to position themselves on the right side of environment and society, as opposed to demonstrations of actually having taken the measures necessary to meaningfully effect change.

Of course, the term ESG can be used the same way—especially when it comes to its social and governance aspects which have enjoyed less objectivity relative to environmental factors. Yet ESG comes with tools missing from "Green" and "sustainability": measurable data. It's why when I founded Measurabl I chose to focus on ESG rather than sustainability or Green, and to help real estate companies collect, track, and act upon their data—one of the most valuable tools at their disposal.

We have come a long way from those early aspirational ideas of saving the environment to a point where we can define what is needed to be carbon neutral, or even just to perform efficiently as businesses.

ESG is a set of metrics that lead us to more reliable returns with less risk.

It's worth burying the notion that including ESG metrics in business decisions is no longer a fringe concept. Consider the seminal 2019 announcement by the Business Roundtable—an association of leading American CEOs with 20 million employees and over USD $9 trillion in annual revenue—that their view on the purpose of a corporation would no longer merely be for shareholder returns, but the benefit of all stakeholders. It was one in a cascade of pronouncements by business organizations around the world that reduces to the common refrain that good business is also good for the environment and society broadly. That constitutes the new "bottom line".

I work to bring about a world where capital flows virtuously to buildings that improve our environment and society. This is a world where not just one or two out of twenty buildings monitor and disclose ESG performance but every building, everywhere. Measurabl exists to enable and pull forward this reality.

In 2018, the U.S. Energy Information Administration's Commercial Buildings Energy Consumption Survey (CBECS) estimated there were 5.9 million office buildings in the United States. That same year, around 67,200 of these buildings had LEED certification—barely more than 1%. If we are to believe that Green certifications are our path towards sustainable real estate, then we are clearly well-off track.

But let's turn this concept on its head. As opposed to certifying a miniscule slice of the world's buildings as "Green," imagine instead that all buildings are on a spectrum of "more or less sustainable" and that their status can be measured. Our task, then, is to make that status *transparent* as opposed to labeling the lucky few.

Transparency makes owners more accountable to tenants, investors, and regulators. But perhaps most importantly, building owners and operators will have the information they need to manage their buildings towards the optimal state objectively. This is the direction the industry needs to head toward: objective measurement and disclosure for *all* buildings, not subjective labeling for the few.

There is much work to be done to bring about transparency of this scale. Real estate is, after all, well known as opaque. That makes this idea all the more exciting: that the real estate sector can be a leader in environmental and social transparency instead of its adversary.

It is possible.

The magic elixir? Readily accessible, investment-grade ESG data. Putting this information alongside traditional financial metrics will allow the people who make decisions about how to buy, sell, lease, appraise, insure, and finance real estate to do their job better.

It is also eminently doable right now.

That's because the real estate industry has a great advantage over most other asset classes: it is inherently measurable because virtually every structure on the planet has utility meters recording energy consumption and therefore, carbon emissions. We can and should start with making that preexisting data easy to access and comparable across buildings. We can grow the mixture of metrics to include water, waste, capex, and so on from there. Many of these metrics are also preexisting and just need to be captured and structured.

The ecosystem of real estate developers, operators, owners, and tenants works better roughly proportional to its access to information. These improvements are contingent on data being granular enough, complete enough, and timely enough to be *easily* shared and understood by all stakeholders in a real estate transaction. It must also cover the entire building universe, not just one or two percent of buildings, for example, those certified to one of the many dozens of voluntary Green standards.

A sustainable future is therefore predicated on enablement of the entire real estate sector having better, more transparent ESG information.

My experience these last 14 years gives me confidence we will get there. Since I started Measurabl, an ESG technology company, in 2013, the market has evolved substantially the way I had hoped. Environmental science, government policy, stakeholder capitalism, and technology are intersecting in delightful ways and elevating to their rightful place in the real estate business. Social issues such as equality, health, and wellbeing are understood as issues important for real estate stakeholders like tenants and investors. Diversity, equity, and inclusion are matters of good governance.

These things were *not* obvious in 2013. Information asymmetry, if not flat-out derision for ESG information, were status quo. It's a remarkable shift in less than a decade.

With the climate crisis omnipresent and social dislocation rife, ESG has become the essential and powerful business toolkit for addressing them head on. These new corporate, social, and investment philosophies are transforming markets far beyond real estate by adding more and better information into the decision equation, moving us substantially closer to more informed and effective markets.

Footnotes

Chapter 1

[1] "5 Years Ago Bernie Madoff Was Sentenced to 150 Years In Prison – Here's How His Scheme Worked," Yang S, Business Insider, Jul 1 2014

[2] Speech by Dianne Feinstein, United States Senator from California, introducing a bill to direct the Agency for International Development to carry out a pilot program to promote the production and use of fuel-efficient stoves. Congressional Record Volume 155, Number 99 (Monday, July 6, 2009)

[3] "84% of investors apply, or are considering, ESG – Morgan Stanley," Kilroy M, Pensions & Investment Jun 18 2018

[4] "How to take the long-term view in a short-term world," Murray S, Financial Times, Feb 25 2021

[5] "Trends in the Fashion Industry. The Perception of Sustainability and Circular Economy: A Gender/Generation Quantitative Approach," Gazzola P, Pavione E, Pezzetti R, Grechi D, Sustainability, 12, 2020

[6] "Barriers towards a systemic change in the clothing industry: How do sustainable fashion enterprises influence their sector?" Molderez I and Van Elst B, The Journal of Corporate Citizenship, No. 57, New Business Models for Sustainable Fashion, Mar 2015

[7] "The rise in ESG ratings: What's the score?" Malik Chua J, Vogue Business, Oct 28 2020

[8] "The Investor Revolution: Shareholders are getting serious about sustainability," Eccles RG and Klimenko S, Harvard Business Review, May-June 2019

[9] "Majority of ESG funds outperform wider market over 10 years," Riding S, Financial Times, Jun 13, 2020

[10] "Real Estate Predictions 2020 | Article 7 Real estate in 2020: the year climate change bears down on investment pricing," Deloitte white paper, 2020

[11] "White Paper on Sustainability: A Report on the Green Building Movement," Building Design & Construction, Nov 2003

[12] "Thoughts during the Building Research Establishment's 75th Anniversary," Atkinson G, Construction History, Vol. 12 (1996), pp. 101-107

[13] "Green Architecture," Wines J, Taschen, 2000

[14] "Four Decades of Green Design," Flynn K, Architect Magazine, Dec 3 2019

[15] EPA website (https://www.epa.gov/smartgrowth/location-and-green-building) (accessed Mar 26 2021)

[16] "The troubling evolution of corporate greenwashing," Watson B, The Guardian, Aug 20, 2016

[17] "Greenwashing: What Your Client Should Know to Avoid Costly Litigation and Consumer Backlash," Diffenderfer M and Baker KC, Natural Resources & Environment, Vol. 25, No. 3 (Winter 2011), pp. 21-25

[18] "What is emissions trading?," The Guardian, Jul 5, 2011

[19] "The Political History of Cap and Trade," Conniff R, Smithsonian Magazine, August 2009.

[20] "The Curious Case of Greening in Carbon Markets," Boyd W and Salzman J, Environmental Law, Vol. 41, No. 1 (Winter 2011), pp. 73-94

[21] "Carbon credits undercut climate change actions says report," McGrath M, BBC, Aug 25, 2015

[22] "G-8 Failure Reflects U.S. Failure on Climate Change," Hansen J, Huffington Post, Aug 9, 2009

[23] "No longer termed a 'failure,' California's cap-and-trade program faces a new critique: Is it too successful?," Hiltzik M, Los Angeles Times, Jan 12, 2018

[24] "Bottom Line on Offsets," Goodward J and Kelly A, World Resources Institute, August 2010

[25] "Greenwash: Are carbon offsetters taking us for a ride?" Pearce F, Dec 11 2008, The Guardian

[26] "Indulgences in Late Medieval England: Passports to Paradise?" Swanson RN, 2007 Cambridge University Press

[27] "Accounting for forest carbon pool dynamics in product carbon footprints: Challenges and opportunities," Newell JP and Vos RO, Environmental Impact Assessment Review, Volume 37, Nov 2012, pp 23-36

[28] "How buyers can guard themselves from 'greenwashing'," Harney KR, The Washington Post, Jan 10 2018

[29] "Sustainability-linked bond market to swell up to $150 billion: JPMorgan ESG DCM head," Ranasinghe D, Reuter's, Mar 22, 2021

[30] "Obstacles to developing sustainable cities: the real estate rigidity trap," Turner V K, Ecology and Society, Vol. 22, No. 2 (Jun 2017)

[31] "Report of the World Commission on Environment and Development: Our Common Future," United Nations World Commission on Environment and Development, 1987

[32] United Nations Sustainability Goals website (https://sdgs.un.org/) (accessed 3/19/21)

[33] "Green building: Improving the lives of billions by helping to achieve the UN Sustainable Development Goals," World Green Building Council website ((https://www.worldgbc.org/news-media/green-building-improving-lives-billions-helping-achieve-un-sustainable-development-goals) accessed 3/19/2021)

[34] "Toward a Methodological Critique of Sustainable Development," Jacob M, The Journal of Developing Areas, Vol. 28, No. 2, Jan 1994

[35] "What Is the SEC's Edgar?" Wall Street Journal, Sep 21 2017

[36] "25 Years Ago I Coined the Phrase "Triple Bottom Line." Here's Why It's Time to Rethink It," Elkington J, Harvard Business Review, Jun 25 2018

[37] Corporate sustainability: historical development and reporting practices, Christofi A, Christofi P, Sisaye S, Management Research Review, Vol. 35 No. 2, 2012

[38] "Northern Trust unveils industry-first sustainable real estate index," EFT Strategy, Feb 1 2017

[39] "Obstacles to developing sustainable cities: the real estate rigidity trap," Turner V K, Ecology and Society, Vol. 22, No. 2, Jun 2017

[40] "Obstacles to developing sustainable cities: the real estate rigidity trap," Turner V K, Ecology and Society, Vol. 22, No. 2, Jun 2017

[41] "Sustainable real estate development: the dynamics of market penetration," Goering J, Journal of Sustainable Real Estate, Vol. 1, 2009

[42] "Making it easy to be green: using impact fees to encourage green building," Kingsley B, New York University Law Review 83 (2), 2008

[43] "The Annals of the University of Oradea Economic Sciences, Tom XXVIII 2019," Issue 2, Dec 2019, ISSN 1222-569X

[44] *United States Supreme Court: TSC Industries v. Northway, Inc.* (426 U.S. 438 (1976)), and Securities and Exchange Commission Code of Federal Regulations 4 C.F.R. 229.303

[45] "Business Roundtable Redefines the Purpose of a Corporation to Promote 'An Economy That Serves All Americans'," press statement from the Business Roundtable, Aug 19 2019

[46] "Group of top CEOs says maximizing shareholder profits no longer can be the primary goal of corporations," McGregor J, Washington Post, Aug 19 2019

[47] "Defining CSR: Problems and Solutions," Sheehy B, Journal of Business Ethics, Vol 131, 2015

[48] "A History of Corporate Social Responsibility: Concepts and Practices," Carroll A, The Oxford Handbook of Corporate Social Responsibility, 2008

[49] "Community Fair Trade," Body Shop Website (www.thebodyshop.com/en-us/about-us/brand-values/community-fair-trade/a/a00009) (accessed Nov 24, 2021)

[50] "How the Social Mission of Ben & Jerry's Survived Being Gobbled Up," Gelles D, New York Times, Aug 21 2015

[51] "The Social Responsibility of Business is to Increase its Profits," Friedman M, The New York Times Magazine, Sep 13 1970

[52] "Stop Talking About How CSR Helps Your Bottom Line," Meier S and Cassar L, Harvard Business Review, Jan 31 2018

[53] "Corporate Social Responsibility (CSR): Theory and Practice in a Developing Country Context," Jamali D and Mirshak R, Journal of Business Ethics, Vol 72, 2007

[54] "Strategy and Society: The Link Between Competitive Advantage and Corporate Social Responsibility," Porter M, Harvard Business Review, Dec 2006

[55] "Stop Talking About How CSR Helps Your Bottom Line," Meier S and Cassar L, Harvard Business Review, Jan 31 2018

[56] "Who Cares Wins — Connecting Financial Markets to a Changing World," International Finance Corporation, Oct 2005

[57] "A legal framework for the integration of environmental, social and governance issues into institutional investment, produced for the Asset Management Working Group of the UNEP Finance Initiative," Freshfields Bruckhaus Deringer, Oct 2005

[58] "ESG Investing: Practices, Progress and Challenges", Boffo R and Patalano R, OECD Paris 2020

[59] "An Evolution in ESG Indexing," Kjellberg S, Pradhan T, Kuh T, BlackRock iShares whitepaper (2019)

[60] "An Evolution in ESG Indexing," Kjellberg S, Pradhan T, Kuh T, BlackRock iShares whitepaper (2019)

[61] "New Evidence on the Green Building Rent and Price Premium," Fuerst F and McAllister P, paper presented at the Annual Meeting of the American Real Estate Society, Monterey, CA, April 3, 2009.

Chapter 2

[1] "The shareholders putting sustainability on the agenda," Berridge R, The Guardian, Apr 15 2013

[2] "ESG Investing: The Growth Opportunity That Most Advisors Miss," Lundquist S, Wealth Management Magazine, Oct 10 2017

[3] "BofA Merrill Lynch Global Research's ESG in equities investing study," UNPRI website, 2 Mar 2018 (https://www.unpri.org/fixed-income/bofa-merrill-lynch-global-researchs-esg-in-equities-investing-study/2742.article) (accessed Mar 31 2021)

[4] "90% of investors think ESG portfolios perform as well or better than non-ESG," Baker S, Pensions & Investments, Oct 2 2018

[5] "Majority of ESG funds outperform wider market over 10 years," Riding S, The Financial Times, Jun 13 2020

[6] "ESG index funds hit $250 billion as pandemic accelerates impact investing boom," Stevens P, CNBC.com, Sep 2 2020

[7] BlackRock analysis of data from Simfund, Broadridge and GBI (as of November 2020). Closed-end funds, funds of funds excluded, and Money Market funds included.

[8] "ESG Disclosure Rules From Europe Challenge U.S. Fund Managers," Eaglesham J and Hirtenstein A, The Wall Street Journal, Mar 22 2021

[9] Blackstone Responsible Investing Policy, Sep 2019 (https://www.blackstone.com/docs/default-source/black-papers/bx-responsible-investing-policy.pdf?sfvrsn=cef0a3ad_2) (accessed Apr 5 2021)

[10] PGGM website (https://www.pggm.nl/en/our-services/esg-integration/) (accessed Apr 5 2021)

[11] CalPERS Strategic Plan 2017–22, p6 (https://www.calpers.ca.gov/docs/forms-publications/2017-22-strategic-plan.pdf) (accessed Apr 5 2021)

[12] "Larry Fink's 2021 letter to CEOs," BlackRock website (https://www.blackrock.com/corporate/investor-relations/larry-fink-ceo-letter) (accessed Mar 31 2021)

[13] "The ETF market will hit $50 trillion by 2030, Bank of America says," Reinicke C, Business Insider, Dec 13 2019

[14] "U.S. ETF market tops $5 trillion in assets as investors stampede into stocks on vaccine hopes," Pisani B, CNBC, Nov 17 2020

[15] "ESG and Active ETFs Witnessed Unprecedented Inflows in 2020" Chen M, ETF Trends, Jan 11 2021

[16] Case Study on Measurabl, inc website (https://www.measurabl.com/resources/corestate-capital-launches-esg-initiatives-and-prepares-for-whats-ahead/) (accessed Mar 22 2021)

[17] Case Study on Measurabl, inc website (https://f.hubspotusercontent30.net/hubfs/565185/_Marketing%20C ollateral/Case%20Studies/CaseStudy_GTIS.pdf) (accessed Mar 22 2021)

[18] Press release from GTIS Partners LP (https://www.businesswire.com/news/home/20200303005702/en/G TIS-Partners-Maintains-Top-Spots-in-GRESB-Sustainability-Ranking) (accessed Mar 24 2021)

[19] Press release from New World Development Company Limited Hong Kong, Jan 8 2021 (https://finance.yahoo.com/news/world-development-becomes-worlds-first-082900413.html)

[20] "Montage Beverly Hills Sells for Estimated $415 Million," Madans H, Los Angeles Business Journal, Jan 3 2020

[21] Press release from Ohana Real Estate Investors, Mar 21 2021 (https://www.prnewswire.com/news-releases/ohana-real-estate-investors-early-esg-commitments-pay-off-for-luxury-hospitality-portfolio-301254553.html)

[22] AccountAbility website (https://www.accountability.org/insights/7-esg-trends-for-2021-and-beyond-accountabilitys-predictions/) (accessed Mar 19 2021)

[23] "Origins of Shareholder Activism," Koppell J (Ed), Palgrave Macmillan, (Jan 12 2011)

[24] "Reasonable Investor(s)," Lin TCW, 95 Boston University Law Review, 461, (2015)

[25] "Activist investor takes a big stake in AT&T, pushing for spinoffs and major changes," La Monica PR, CNN, Sep 9 2019

[26] "Elliott eyes Hyundai restructuring for next chaebol battle," Financial Times, Mar 14 2019

[27] "Disney Activist Loeb Urges Using Dividend to Fund Streaming," Deveau S, Bloomberg, Oct 7 2020

[28] "Microsoft names Satya Nadella its next CEO," Martin S, U.S.A Today, Feb 4 2014

[29] "U.S. activist fund becomes largest Rolls-Royce shareholder," Financial Times, Jul 31 2015

[30] "Why can Burger King, but not Wendy's, own Hortons?" Cox R, Reuter's, Aug 26 2014

[31] "Top 10 Activist Investors in the U.S.," Investopedia, Oct 20 2020 (https://www.investopedia.com/top-10-activist-investors-in-the-us-5083258) (accessed Apr 6 2021)

[32] "Deep Value: Why Activist Investors and Other Contrarians Battle for Control of Losing Corporations," Carlisle T, Wiley Finance, 2014, p4

[33] "The Activism of Carl Icahn and Bill Ackman," blog post by Tonello M of the Conference Board on Harvard Law School Forum on   Corporate   governance,

(https://corpgov.law.harvard.edu/2014/05/29/the-activism-of-carl-icahn-and-bill-ackman/) (accessed Apr 6 2021)

[34] "Corporate upgraders: America should make life easier, not harder, for activist investors," the Economist, Feb 15 2014

[35] Letter from JANA Partners & CalSTRS to Apple, Inc. Jan 16 2018

[36] "Apple should address youth phone addiction, two large investors say," CNBC.com, Jan 8 2018

[37] "Why an Activist Hedge Fund Cares Whether Apple's Devices Are Bad for Kids,", Eccles RG, Harvard Business Review, Jan 16 2018

[38] "A Capitalist Repents: Jeff Ubben Is Out to Make Things Right," Hammond E, Bloomberg, Sep 16 2020

[39] "Analysis: New ESG Hedge Fund Tops Activist List in Third Quarter," Dhanasarnsombat S, Bloomberg Law, Nov 5 2020 *Note: The campaigns were inherited from ValueAct Spring Fund, which was rolled out as part of the launch of Inclusive Capital Partners

[40] "World's Top Carbon Offenders Need to Step Up, Says Investor Group," Min S, CIO Magazine, Mar 22 2021

[41] "Dutch investors raise climate change activism," Preesman L, Investment & Pensions Europe, Nov 6 2008

[42] 2015 data from Activist Insight (https://www.activistinsight.com/research/AI_SRZShareholderActivismInTheUK_121115054552.pdf)

[43] "Climate risk assessment in global real estate investing," PGGM whitepaper 2019

[44] SEC 13F filings (https://sec.report/CIK/0001394096) (accessed Apr 6 2021)

[45]   Zevin   Impact   Report   June   2020 (https://static1.squarespace.com/static/5d0cee8d37a63200017a0906/t/5f0dbb8ed95d7b59b3574d41/1594735507499/Zevin+Impact+Report+June+2020.pdf) (accessed Apr 6 2021)

[46]   Zevin   Impact   Report   September   2018 (https://static1.squarespace.com/static/5d0cee8d37a63200017a0906/t/5dc98714f357fb004ea018ef/1573488427444/Impact+Report+2018.pdf) (accessed Apr 6 2021)

[47] "Shareholder activists poised for a resurgence in 2021," White and Case   note   to   clients,   Mar   1   2021 (https://www.lexology.com/library/detail.aspx?g=9129f767-4f99-4cbf-b11f-112ed748552a) (accessed Apr 6 2021)

[48] "New Tactics and ESG Themes Take Shareholder Activism in New Directions," Skadden, Arps, Slate, Meagher & Flom LLP note to clients, Feb 12 2021 (https://www.jdsupra.com/legalnews/new-tactics-and-esg-themes-take-7787288/) (accessed Apr 6 2021)

[49]   Net   Zero   Asset   Managers   website (https://www.netzeroassetmanagers.org/#) (accessed Apr 4 2021)

[50] "Net Zero asset managers now represent one-third of global assets," Bradford H, Pensions & Investments, Mar 29 2021

[51] "Sustainability chief calls for more transparency as companies eye net-zero emissions," Bucak S, Citywire Apr 5 2021

[52] "Carbon Markets: A Hidden Value Source for Commercial Real Estate?" Binkley A, Ciochetti B, The Journal of Sustainable Real Estate, Vol. 2 No. 1, 2010

[53] "2019 Global Status Report for Buildings and Construction," prepared by the International Energy Agency for the United Nations Environment Programme, 2019

[54] "Dramatic growth in laws to protect environment, but widespread failure to enforce, finds report," press release from the United Nations

Environment Program, Jan 24 2019 (https://www.unep.org/news-and-stories/press-release/dramatic-growth-laws-protect-environment-widespread-failure-enforce) (accessed Apr 12)

[55] "Biden Budget Seeks $1.4 Billion to Target Environmental Justice," Scott D, Bloomberg Law, Apr 9 2021

[56] U.S. Department of Energy's Energy Codes website (https://www.energycodes.gov/status-state-energy-code-adoption) (accessed Apr 22 2021)

[57] California Government's Building Standards Commission webpage (https://www.dgs.ca.gov/BSC/Resources/Page-Content/Building-Standards-Commission-Resources-List-Folder/CALGreen) (accessed Apr 24 2021)

[58] "LL87: Energy Audits & Retro-commissioning," New York City Mayor's Office of Sustainability website (https://www1.nyc.gov/html/gbee/html/plan/ll87.shtml) (accessed Apr 29 2021)

[59] "Directive 2010/31/EU of the European Parliament and of the Council of 19 May 2010, on the energy performance of buildings," Official Journal of the European Union, Jun 2010

[60] "EU countries back green building renovations, but quiet on binding standards – draft," Abnett K, Reuters, Feb 22 2021

[61] "SEC Announces Enforcement Task Force Focused on Climate and ESG Issues," Securities and Exchange Commission press release, Mar 4 2021 (https://www.sec.gov/news/press-release/2021-42) (accessed Mar 5 2021)

[62] "ESG Disclosure Rules From Europe Challenge U.S. Fund Managers," Eaglesham J and Hirtenstein A, The Wall Street Journal, Mar 22 2021

[63] "A Climate for Change: Meeting Investor Demand for Climate and ESG Information at the SEC," speech by Acting SEC Chair Allison

Herren Lee, Washington D.C., Mar 15 2021 (https://www.sec.gov/news/speech/lee-climate-change) (accessed Apr 6 2021)

[64] "Measuring Stakeholder Capitalism: Towards Common Metrics and Consistent Reporting of Sustainable Value Creation," World Economic Forum website (https://www.weforum.org/reports/measuring-stakeholder-capitalism-towards-common-metrics-and-consistent-reporting-of-sustainable-value-creation) (accessed May 2 2021)

[65] "Ethical dilemmas put company lawyers in the spotlight," Love B, Financial Times, Jun 25 2020

[66] "Overselling Sustainability Reporting," Pucker KP, Harvard Business Review, May-Jun 2021

[67] "Energy Saving Performance Contracts," Johnson RL, The Military Engineer, Vol. 97, No. 638 (Nov-Dec 2005

[68] "Going-Going-Green: Strategies for fostering Sustainable New Federal Buildings," Tolan PE, Public Contract Law Journal, Vol 41 No 2 Winter, 2012

[69] Energy Policy Act 1992, 106 Stat. 2846 Public Law 102-486, Oct 24 1992

[70] "Greening the Government Through Efficient Energy Management," Executive Order (EO) 13123, Jun 3 1999

[71] "Strengthening Federal Environmental, Energy, and Transportation Management," Executive Order (EO) 13423, Jan 24 2007

[72]"Planning for Federal Sustainability in the Next Decade," Executive Order (EO) 13693, Mar 19 2015

[73] "GSA Raises Federal Building Requirement to LEED Gold," Architect Magazine, Nov 1 2010

[74] "How Real Estate Pros Can Prepare For Future Environmental Regulations," Forbes Real Estate Council, Forbes, Feb 22 2021

[75] "Legal collaboration led to PG&E deal for victims of wildfires," Love B, Financial Times, Dec 10 2020

[76] "Final Insured Losses for Australian Bushfires of 2019/2020 Estimated at A$1.866B," Insurance Journal, Jan 6, 2021

[77] "Las Vegas pushes to become first to ban ornamental grass," The Ledger Independent, Apr 12 2021

[78] "Your Building Can Make You Sick or Keep You Well," Allen JG, New York Times Mar 4 2020

[79] "Nauset Completes Critical Building Upgrades as COVID-19 Persists," Boston Real Estate Times, Apr 14 2021

[80] "Real estate: Big Santa Clara building ready for tenants with COVID bells and whistles," Avalos G, Mercury News, Apr 15 2021

[81] "Roadmap to Improve and Ensure Good Indoor Ventilation in the Context of COVID-19," World Health Organization, Mar 1 2021

[82] "COVID-19: Are Building Managers Measuring the Right Air Quality Parameters?," Diehl D, Buildings Magazine, Feb 3 2021

[83] "How Smart Environments Will Take Shape Post-COVID-19," Rosencrance L, IoT World Today, Apr 14 2021

[84] "Black Lives Matter Movement," Howard University School of Law Library   website (https://library.law.howard.edu/civilrightshistory/BLM) (accessed Apr 2 2021)

[85] "Black Lives Matter May Be the Largest Movement in U.S. History," Buchanan L, Bui Q, Patel JK, New York Times, Jul 3 2020

[86] "As Pandemic Deaths Add Up, Racial Disparities Persist—And In Some Cases Worsen," Wood D, NPR Sep 23 2020

[87] "'Black Lives Matter' is About More than the Police," Cullors P, American Civil Liberties Union website, Jun 23 2020 (https://www.aclu.org/news/criminal-law-reform/black-lives-matter-is-about-more-than-the-police/) (accessed Apr 4 2020)

[88] "How Systemic Racism Exists In U.S. Housing Policies," LeBlanc A, Forbes, Jul 9 2020

[89] "Landlord trying to swap renters for 'rich, white tenants': suit," Algar S, New York Post, Sep 9 2014

[90] "Black Real Estate Agent Program launched to support aspiring Black agents," Baltimore Times, Apr 16 2021

[91] "Black homeownership rate hits lowest level since the 1960s—that's unlikely to change in Pandemic Year 2," Passey J, MarketWatch, Mar 10 2021

[92] "Small Business Green Recovery Fund to power U.S. climate transition," Lashitew A, Report, Brookings Institute, Mar 1 2021 (https://www.brookings.edu/research/small-business-green-recovery-fund-to-power-us-climate-transition/) (accessed Apr 10 2021)

[93] "European Union unveils recovery fund financing plan," Reuters, Apr 14 2021

[94] "Development trend and segmentation of the U.S. green building market: corporate perspective on green contractors and design firms," Han Y, He T, Chang R, Xue R, Journal of Construction Engineering and Management, ASCE, 146(11), 1-14, 2020

Chapter 3

[1] BOMA 360 website (https://www.boma.org/BOMA/Recognition-Awards/BOMA_360_Performance.aspx) (Accessed May 30, 2021)

[2] BOMA website (https://www.boma.org/BOMA/Recognition-Awards/BOMA_360_Performance.aspx) (Accessed May 30, 2021)

[3] BOMA 360 website (https://boma360.secure-platform.com/a/page/office-criteria) (Accessed May 30, 2021)

[4] "Single Stream User Guide," BOMA Canada Website (http://www.bestsustainablebuildings.org/wp-content/uploads/2019/03/User-Guide-Single-Stream.pdf) (Accessed May 30, 2021)

[5] BOMA Canada website (http://bomacanada.ca/bomabest/fees/) (Accessed May 30, 2021)

[6] BREEM website (https://tools.breeam.com/filelibrary/BREEAM%20In%20Use/KN5 686---BREEAM-In-Use-White-Paper_dft2.pdf) (Accessed May 30, 2021)

[7] Energy Star website (https://www.energystar.gov/buildings/building_recognition/building _certification) (Accessed May 30, 2021)

[8] Energy Star website (https://www.energystar.gov/buildings/about_us/newsroom/media_f aqs) (Accessed May 30, 2021)

[9] Green Globe website (https://greenglobe.com/standard/) (Accessed May 30, 2021)

[10] Green Building Initiative website (https://thegbi.org/green-globes-certification/what-it-costs/) (Accessed May 30, 2021)

[11] *Gifford et al., v. U.S. Green Building Council et al.*, United States District Court, Southern District of New York, August 15, 2011., 10 Civ 7747 (2010).

[12] "The True Cost of LEED-Certified Green Buildings," Vamosi SJ, HPAC Engineering, Jan 1, 2011

[13] "Sustainable Options: LEED and Green Globes – a Comparison," Randazzo T, Berman Wright website (https://bermanwright.com/sustainable-options-leed-and-green-globes-a-comparison-part-one-of-a-three-part-series/) (Accessed June 1, 2021)

[14] "False Negative Tests for SARS-CoV-2 Infection — Challenges and Implications," Woloshin S, Patel N, Kesselheim AS, New England Journal of Medicine, August 6 2020.

[15] "Seaspiracy: Netflix documentary accused of misrepresentation by participants," McVeigh K, the Guardian, Mar 31 2021

[16] "The Financial Crisis Inquiry Report," The U.S. Financial Crisis Inquiry Commission, Jan 2011

[17] "Report to Congress on Assigned Credit Ratings, As Required by Section 939F of the Dodd-Frank Wall Street Reform and Consumer Protection Act," U.S. Securities and Exchange Commission, Dec 2012

[18] GRESB website (https://gresb.com/2021-2023-annual-fee-schedule/) (Accessed May 30, 2021)

Chapter 4

[1] "The Value and Impact of Building Codes," Vaughan E, Environmental and Energy Study Institute, Sep 30, 2013

[2] "Pure Food: Securing the Federal Food and Drugs Act of 1906," Young, JH, Princeton University Press, 1989

[3] "The Zero-Carbon House: It's Just Around the Corner," Wired Magazine, Aug 22, 2011

[4] "Reinventing Green Building: Why Certification Systems Aren't Working and What We Can Do About It," Yudelson, J, New Society Publishers, 2016

[5] "Breen Building Adoption Index 2019" CBRE p3, 2019

[6] "Green investing 'is definitely not going to work', says ex-BlackRock executive," Rushe, D, The Guardian, Mar 30, 2021

[7] "Corporate Climate Efforts Lack Impact, Say Former Sustainability Executives," Kishan S, Bloomberg, Jul 13 2021

[8] "Overselling Sustainability Reporting," Pucker K, Harvard Business Review, May-June 2021

[9] "Surfside inspectors visited Champlain Towers South dozens of times. Now its collapse is spurring calls for reform," Tolan C, Devine C, CNN, Jul 14 2021

[10] "Changing Winds on Disclosure: What to Expect from Increased ESG Disclosure Requirements," The National Law Review, Vol Xi, No. 28, Jul 14 2021

[11] U.S. Securities and Exchange Commission Asset Management Advisory Committee Recommendations for ESG, Jul 7 2021

[12] "As SEC Chairman Pushes His Attorneys, Some Are Choosing the Door," Love B, National Law Journal, Jul 23 2021

[13] "The Rule of Law," Bingham T, Penguin UK, 2011

[14] "How green are green bonds? Ratings can help investors know," Kiesel F, The Conversation, Sep 8 2019

[15] "How the $1 trillion market for 'green' bonds is changing Wall Street," Miller A, CNBC May 28 2021

[16] "Sustainability integration for sovereign debt investors: engaging with countries on the SDGs," Van Zanten JA, Sharma B, Christensen M, Journal of Sustainable Finance & Investment, 0:0, 2021

[17] "EU launches green bond framework to help it meet climate goals," Jessop S, Reuters, Jul 6 2021

[18] "U.S. Cannabis Sales Hit Record $17.5 Billion As Americans Consume More Marijuana Than Ever Before," Yakowicz W, Forbes, Mar 3 2021

Chapter 5

[1] "Consumers' Response to an On-Shelf Nutrition Labelling System in Supermarkets: Evidence to Inform Policy and Practice," Hobin E, Bollinger B, Sacco J, Liebman E, Vanderlee L, Zuo F, Rosella L, l'Abbe M, Manson H, Hammond D, Milbank Quarterly 95, no. 3, 2017

[2] "Promoting Healthy Choices in Non-Chain Restaurants: Effects of a Simple Cue to Customers," Nothwehr FK, Snetselaar L, Dawson J, Schultz U, Health Promotion Practice, Vol 14 No 1, Jan 2013

[3] "Nudging Energy Efficiency Behavior: The Role of Information Labels," Newell RG, Siikamäki J, Journal of the Association of Environmental and Resource Economists, Vol. 1 No. 4, Dec 2014

[4] "Chlorofluorocarbons and the Depletion of Stratospheric Ozone," Rowland FS, American Scientist, Vol. 77 No. 1, Jan-Feb 1989

[5] "How the Covid-19 Threat Could Help Us Breathe Easier at the Office," Mims C, Wall Street Journal, Sep 4 2021

[6] "Asbestos: Medical and Legal Aspects," Castleman B et. al., Aspen Law & Business, 1996

[7] "$ 9.54 Billion Growth in Global Indoor Air Quality Solutions Market During 2020-2024," Technavio research report, Feb 2 2021

[8] "Economic, Environmental and Health Implications of Enhanced Ventilation in Office Buildings," MacNaughton P, Pegues J, Satish U, Santanam S, Spengler J, Allen J, International Journal of Environmental Research and Public Health, Nov 2015

[9] "Indoor Air Quality and Student Performance: Evidence from A Large Scale Field Study in Primary Schools," Kok N, Duran N, Eichholtz P, Palacios J, Conference Paper, Feb 21 2021

[10] "Diversity, Inequality, and Microsegregation," Tach L., Cityscape, Vol. 16, No. 3, 2014

[11] 26 CFR Part 1 TD 9889 (Internal Revenue Service Final Regulations: Investing in Qualified Opportunity Funds)

[12] "The Significance Of Investing In Opportunity Zones," Rieder E, Forbes, Dec 7 2018.

Made in USA - Kendallville, IN
60588_9798425299970
04.18.2022 1251